DR. OETKER

BEST RECIPES

GERMAN COOKING AND BAKING

DR. OETKER

BEST RECIPES

GERMAN COOKING AND BAKING

Dr. Oetker Verlag

Best recipes FOREWORD

"Best Recipes" contains the best recipes from "German Baking Today" and "German Cooking Today", the most successful standard books on German cookery in the English language.

In it you will find all the typical dishes of Germany, such as goulash soup, herring fillets and knuckle of pork with sauerkraut as well as cakes and pastries including Black Forest cherry gâteau, apple strudel and marble cake.

The numerous recipe photographs, detailed step-by-step photographs and of course the clear precise instructions for the recipes make the book extremely easy to use and user-friendly.

The recipes have been tried and tested in Dr. Oetker's test kitchen to ensure that both beginners and experienced cooks will be successful in making them.

We wish you great pleasure in trying and enjoying the wonderful variety of these German recipes.

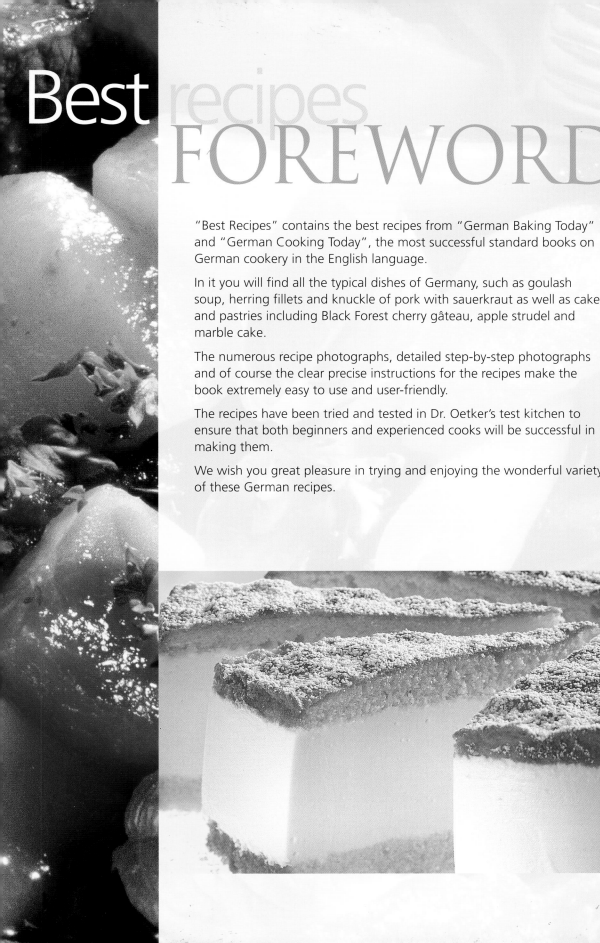

German
COOKING &

Abbreviations

g	=	gram
kg	=	kilogram
l	=	litre
lb	=	pound
ml	=	millilitre
oz	=	ounce
cm	=	centimetre
in	=	inch
P	=	protein
F	=	fat
C	=	carbohydrate
kJ	=	kilojoule
kcal	=	kilocalorie

General information

1 Read the recipe carefully before you start cooking – or, better still, before you buy the ingredients. Often the instructions and the recipe as a whole will become clearer as a result.

2 For best results, follow the quantities given in the recipes on the following pages carefully.

3 Preparation times are approximate and include the times of the actual operations carried out by the cook. Cooling, refrigeration, marinating and standing times as well as the rising times of yeast dough are not included in the preparation times when no other parallel activity is involved. In the baking recipes, preparation times and baking times are indicated separately.

Length

Metric	Imperial	
3 mm	$1/8$	in
5 mm	$3/16$	in
1 cm	$3/8$	in
2 cm	$3/4$	in
2.5 cm	1	in
3 cm	$1 1/8$	in
4 cm	$1 1/2$	in
5 cm	2	in
10 cm	4	in
11 cm	$4 1/2$	in
12 cm	5	in
20 cm	8	in
22 cm	$8 1/2$	in
25 cm	10	in
26 cm	10	in
28 cm	11	in
30 cm	12	in
40 cm	16	in

BAKING

4 The baking temperatures and baking times indicated in the recipes are guidelines which may be increased or reduced depending on the performance of the oven.

5 Always follow the manufacturer's instructions when using the oven. When baking a cake, check whether it is done by inserting a wooden stick towards the end of the baking time indicated in the recipe. If it comes out clean the cake is done.

6 Unless otherwise indicated, the recipes in the cooking section of the book are for four servings. Where different, the number of servings is given in the recipes. In the baking section the number of pieces for the quantities given is also shown in the recipes. The nutritional values given in all the recipes are per serving or per piece.

Important note:
For dishes prepared with raw eggs that are also eaten raw, only use eggs that you know to be fresh. Store prepared food in the refrigerator and consume within 24 hours.

Temperature

Celsius	Fahrenheit	Gas mark
140 °C	275 °F	1
150 °C	300 °F	2
160 °C	325 °F	3
180 °C	350 °F	4
190 °C	375 °F	5
200 °C	400 °F	6
220 °C	425 °F	7
230 °C	450 °F	8
240 °C	475 °F	9

Conversions and American Standard Measurements

Weight

Metric	Imperial	
10 g	$1/3$	oz
15 g	$1/2$	oz
20 g	$3/4$	oz
25 g	1	oz
30 g	1	oz
40 g	$1^1/2$	oz
50 g	2	oz
60 g	2	oz
70 g	3	oz
75 g	3	oz
100 g	$3^1/2$	oz
125 g	$4^1/2$	oz
150 g	5	oz
175 g	6	oz
200 g	7	oz
225 g	8	oz
250 g	9	oz
275 g	$9^1/2$	oz
300 g	10	oz
325 g	11	oz
350 g	12	oz
375 g	13	oz
400 g	14	oz
450 g	16	oz
500 g	18	oz
600 g	$1^1/4$	lb
700 g	$1^1/2$	lb
750 g	$1^1/2$	lb
800 g	$1^3/4$	lb
900 g	2	lb
1 kg	$2^1/4$	lb
1.1 kg	$2^1/2$	lb
1.2 kg	$2^1/2$	lb
1.3 kg	$2^3/4$	lb
1.4 kg	3	lb
1.5 kg	$3^3/8$	lb
2 kg	$4^1/2$	lb
2.5 kg	$5^1/2$	lb
3 kg	$6^1/2$	lb
4 kg	9	lb
5 kg	11	lb

For each recipe, measurements are given in metric and Imperial quantities, with American equivalents where appropriate. Conversions given are inevitably approximate; 1 oz is equivalent to 28.34981 g, so exact conversion would involve unwieldy measurements such as $1^1/16$ oz. Therefore 25 g has normally been rounded up to 1 oz and 30 g has been rounded down to 1 oz.

The table below shows the conversions normally used in the recipes. It is important to use all metric or all Imperial measurements in a recipe, not a mixture of the two. Please note that the metric units are more precise than the Imperial ones. For American measurements of solids, see opposite.

Americans commonly use cups to measure solids, rather than weighing them. A cup holds 8 fluid ounces of liquid but the weight of 1 cup of solid ingredients varies from one ingredient to another.

Liquid

Metric	Imperial		American		Metric	Imperial		American	
5 ml	1	teaspoon			350 ml	12	fl oz	$1^1/2$	cups
10 ml	2	teaspoons			375 ml	12	fl oz	$1^1/2$	cups
15 ml	1	tablespoon			400 ml	14	fl oz	$1^3/4$	cups
30 ml	1	fl oz	$1/8$	cup	500 ml	17	fl oz	$2^1/4$	cups
60 ml	2	fl oz	$1/4$	cup	600 ml	21	fl oz	$2^1/2$	cups
75 ml	3	fl oz	$3/8$	cup	700 ml	24	fl oz	3	cups
125 ml	4	fl oz	$1/2$	cup	800ml	28	fl oz	$3^1/2$	cups
150 ml	5	fl oz	$5/8$	cup	1 l	$1^3/4$	pints	$4^1/2$	cups
175 ml	6	fl oz	$3/4$	cup	1.25 l	$2^1/4$	pints	$5^1/2$	cups
200 ml	7	fl oz	$7/8$	cup	1.5 l	$2^3/4$	pints	7	cups
225 ml	8	fl oz	1	cup	2 l	$3^1/2$	pints	9	cups
300 ml	10	fl oz	$1^1/4$	cups	2.5 l	$4^1/4$	pints	11	cups

Foods that weigh about 8 ounces (225 g) per cup include sugar, butter, rice and other whole grains and beans.
Foods that weigh about 4 ounces (115 g) per cup include flours of all grades, mushrooms and ground almonds.

Note that an American pint has 16 fluid ounces, compared with the Imperial pint that has 20 fluid ounces.

Some cookery exprerssions that differ in British and U.S. terminology

British	American	British	American
almonds, flaked	slivered almonds	icing	frosting
apples, cooking	green apples	icing sugar	confectioners' sugar
aubergine	egg plant	jam	jelly, preserve
baking sheet	cookie sheet	loaf tin	loaf pan
biscuits	cookies	mince, to	to grind
butter, unsalted	sweet butter	mould	mold
cake mixture	cake batter	oatmeal	rolled oats
cake tin	cake pan	offal	variety meats
chocolate, plain	semi-sweet chocolate pieces	omelette	omelet
coconut, desiccated	shredded coconut	pancake	crepe
coriander, fresh	cilantro	pinch	dash
cornflour	cornstarch	pip	seed
courgettes	zucchini	piping bag	decorator's bag
cream, double	heavy or whipping cream	pudding bowl	ovenproof bowl
cream, single	light cream	ring mould	tube pan
curd cheese	farmer's cheese	spring onion	scallion
demerara sugar	light brown sugar	stalk	stem
fat	shortening	stock	broth
flour, plain	all-purpose flour	stone	pit
frying pan	skillet	Swiss roll tin	jelly roll pan
grill, to	to broil	whip or whisk, to	beat
grill pan	broiler tray	wholemeal	wholewheat
kitchen paper	paper towel		

German
COOKING

SOUPS
Pages 16–33

THICK SOUPS
Pages 34–39

MEAT
Pages 40–55

POULTRY
Pages 56–61

GAME
Pages 62–69

FISH & SEAFOOD
Pages 70–79

SAUCES
Pages 80–85

VEGETABLES
Pages 86–101

SALADS
Pages 102–113

POTATOES, RICE & PASTA
Pages 114–131

BAKED DISHES
Pages 132–137

EGG & CURD CHEESE DISHES
Pages 138–143

SNACKS
Pages 144–145

DESSERTS
Pages 146–161

German
BAKING

CAKE MIXTURE
Pages 164–179

YEAST DOUGH
Pages 202–213

ALL-IN-ONE CAKE MIXTURE
Pages 180–185

SPONGE MIXTURE
Pages 214–221

SHORTCRUST PASTRY
Pages 186–201

CHEESE AND OIL CAKE MIXTURE
Pages 222–225

STRUDEL
Pages 226–229

PUFF PASTRY
Pages 230–233

PASTRIES FRIED IN FAT
Pages 234–237

CHRISTMAS PASTRY
Pages 238–245

BREAD
Pages 246–249

Best recipes
COOKING

Chicken stock (photograph, bottom)

Preparation time:
about 2 hours;

6 servings

2 litres/3½ pints (9 cups) water
1 bunch soup vegetables
1 onion
1 prepared boiling chicken,
1–1.5 kg/2¼–3¼ lb,
with giblets
salt
200 g/7 oz cooked asparagus
pieces (canned or bottled)
125 g/4½ oz (¾ cup) cooked
long grain rice
2 tablespoons chopped parsley

Per serving:
P: 32 g, F: 15 g, C: 6 g,
kJ: 1203, kcal: 287

1 Bring the water to the boil in a large saucepan.

2 Meanwhile prepare the soup vegetables. Peel the celeriac and cut out any bad parts. Peel the carrots and cut off the green leaves and tips. Wash the celeriac and carrots and let them drain. Remove the outer leaves of the leeks, cut off the root end and dark green leaves. Cut in half lengthways, wash thoroughly and leave to drain. Cut the prepared ingredients into small pieces. Peel the onion.

3 Wash the chicken and giblets if available under cold running water. Put them in the cooking water. Add 1 teaspoon of salt, bring everything to the boil and skim.

4 Add the soup vegetables and onion to the pan. Simmer uncovered over low heat for about 1½ hours.

5 Then pour the stock through a sieve, skim off any fat and season the stock with salt to taste.

6 Take the meat off the bones, remove the skin and cut the meat into small pieces. Add the meat, asparagus pieces and rice to the stock and heat them through.

7 Sprinkle the soup with parsley and serve.

Tip: You can also serve the chicken soup with cooked egg garnish (right of photograph), semolina dumplings (left of photograph), or meatballs (top of photograph) as garnishes.
If you prepare the chicken soup up to and including point 5 on the day before it is to be eaten and leave it to cool, the fat will have solidified by the next day and you can simply remove it with a spoon.
Chicken soup without garnishes can be frozen.
Instead of canned or bottled asparagus you can also use cooked frozen asparagus.
125 g/4½ oz (¾ cup) cooked rice corresponds to about 50 g/2 oz (¼ cup) of uncooked rice.

Goulash soup

Preparation time:
about 80 minutes

300 g/10 oz braising beef,
e.g. shoulder
40 g/1½ oz margarine
or 3 tablespoons cooking oil,
e.g. sunflower oil
1 litre/1¾ pints (4½ cups) meat
stock
200 g/7 oz onions
1 clove garlic
1 yellow and 1 green pepper,
each weighing 200 g/7 oz
200 g/7 oz tomatoes
2 slightly rounded tablespoons
tomato purée
salt
freshly ground pepper
strong paprika powder
½ teaspoon ground caraway
dried marjoram
a few dashes of Tabasco sauce

Per serving:
P: 18 g, F: 15 g, C: 9 g,
kJ: 1011, kcal: 241

1 Rinse the beef under cold running water, pat dry and cut into cubes of 1.5–2 cm/½–¾ in. Melt the margarine or heat the oil in a pan. Brown the cubes of meat thoroughly on all sides in the margarine or oil. Add the meat stock and bring to the boil. Cover and cook over medium heat for about 40 minutes.

2 Meanwhile, peel the onions and cut into slices. Peel the cloves of garlic and dice finely. Cut the peppers in half. Remove the stalks and seeds as well as the white pith inside. Wash the peppers and cut into pieces.

3 Wash the tomatoes, leave to drain and make cross-shaped incisions in the ends. Scald briefly in boiling water and dip into cold water. Peel the tomatoes, remove the stalks and cut the tomatoes into quarters.

4 Add the prepared vegetables and tomato purée to the soup. Season the soup with salt, pepper, paprika powder, caraway and marjoram. Bring back to the boil, cover and cook for another 15 minutes or so.

5 Season the soup with salt, pepper, paprika and Tabasco sauce to taste.

Tip: Goulash soup is suitable for freezing. Instead of fresh tomatoes you can also use a can of peeled tomatoes (drained weight 250 g/9 oz). You can also use ready-cubed meat.
Accompaniment: Nourishing country bread, rye bread or seeded grain rolls.

Pea soup with little sausages

Preparation time:
about 80 minutes

250 g/9 oz dried peas
1.5 litres/2¾ pints (7 cups) water
250 g/9 oz streaky bacon (in one piece)
1 bunch soup vegetables
250 g/9 oz floury boiling potatoes
3 rounded teaspoons bouillon powder
1 teaspoon dried marjoram
1 onion
15 g/½ oz (1 tablespoon) butter
salt
freshly ground pepper
4 Vienna sausages
3–4 teaspoons chopped chives

Per serving:
P: 39 g, F: 31 g, C: 39 g,
kJ: 2479, kcal: 592

1 Put the peas in a sieve, rinse in cold water and put in a large sauce-pan with the water. Bring to the boil and add the bacon. Cover and cook for about 40 minutes over medium heat.

2 Meanwhile, prepare the soup vegetables. Peel the celeriac and cut out any bad parts. Peel the carrots and cut off the green leaves and tips. Wash the celeriac and carrots and let them drain. Remove the outer leaves of the leeks, cut off the root ends and dark green leaves. Cut in half lengthways, wash thoroughly and leave to drain. Wash the potatoes, then peel and rinse them. Slice or dice all the vegetables.

3 Add the bouillon powder, soup vegetables, potatoes and marjoram to the soup. Bring to the boil again, cover and cook for another 20 minutes. Peel and chop the onion. Melt the butter in a pan, add the chopped onion and brown lightly while stirring.

4 Remove the bacon from the soup, chop and return to the soup together with the fried chopped onion. Season with salt, pepper and bouillon powder.

5 Slice the Vienna sausages, add to the soup and heat them through. Sprinkle with chopped chives and serve.

Cream of trout soup

Preparation time:
about 20 minutes

375 g/13 oz smoked trout fillets
50 g/2 oz (4 tablespoons) butter
35 g/1¼ oz (5 tablespoons) plain (all-purpose) flour
750 ml/1¼ pints (3½ cups) vegetable or fish stock
250 ml/8 fl oz (1 cup) whipping cream
4 tablespoons white wine
2–3 teaspoons Worcestershire sauce
salt, pepper, lemon juice
2 tablespoons chopped parsley

Per serving:
P: 23 g, F: 34 g, C: 10 g,
kJ: 1888, kcal: 451

1 Cut the trout fillets into pieces and remove any bones that remain.

2 Melt the butter in a pan. Stir in the flour and cook while still stirring until the mixture has turned light yellow. Pour in the hot stock and stir vigorously using a whisk, making sure that there are no lumps. Bring the mixture to the boil and cook uncovered over a low heat for about 3 minutes, stirring occasionally.

3 Now add the cream, white wine and Worcestershire sauce. Season the soup with salt, pepper and a little lemon juice and bring to the boil again. Add the fish pieces and heat briefly in the soup.

4 Sprinkle the soup with parsley.

Cream of asparagus soup

Preparation time:
about 45 minutes

500 g/18 oz white asparagus
1 litre/1¾ pints (4½ cups) water
salt
sugar
60 g/2 oz (4 tablespoons) butter
about 300 ml/10 fl oz (1¼ cups)
milk
30 g/1 oz (4 tablespoons) plain
(all-purpose) flour
freshly ground white pepper
grated nutmeg
2 egg yolks of medium eggs
2 tablespoons whipping cream
3–4 teaspoons chopped parsley

Per serving:
P: 7 g, F: 21 g, C: 12 g,
kJ: 1117, kcal: 267

1 Wash the asparagus and peel carefully starting from the top and going downward, making sure that all the skin is removed but without damaging the tips. Cut off the lower ends and remove any woody parts. Reserve the peelings and ends. Rinse the asparagus and cut into pieces 3 cm/1¼ in long.

2 Fill a saucepan with 1 litre/1¾ pints (4½ cups) water. Add 1 level teaspoon salt and 20 g/¾ oz (1½ tablespoons) butter. Add the asparagus ends and peelings, bring to the boil, cover and cook for about 15 minutes over medium heat.

3 Strain this stock through a sieve, reserve the cooking liquid and bring back to the boil. Add the pieces of asparagus and bring to the boil. Cover and cook the asparagus for 10–12 minutes until cooked al dente.

4 Put the asparagus pieces in a sieve to drain and again reserve the cooking juices. Add milk to make up the quantity to 1 litre/1¾ pints (4½ cups).

5 Melt the remaining butter in a saucepan. Stir in the flour and continue stirring until the mixture turns light yellow. Add the measured amount of liquid to the mixture and stir vigorously with a whisk, making sure that there are no lumps. Bring the soup to the boil and cook uncovered for about 5 minutes over low heat, stirring occasionally.

6 Season the soup with salt, sugar, pepper and nutmeg. Stir the egg yolk into the cream and slowly add to the soup, stirring carefully to obtain a smooth, even mixture. Do not let the soup boil again. Add the asparagus pieces to the soup and heat them through. Sprinkle with parsley and serve.

Thuringian vegetable soup

Preparation time:
about 75 minutes
excluding defrosting time

500 g/18 oz fresh or frozen
chicken trimmings (pieces of
back, necks, wings)
1 bunch soup vegetables
1.25 litre/2¼ pints (5½ cups)
water
salt
1 bay leaf
3 grains allspice
250 g/9 oz carrots
200 g/7 oz kohlrabi
150 g/5 oz mangetout peas
150 g/5 oz green beans
1 bunch chervil
200 ml/7 fl oz (⅞ cup) whipping
cream
freshly ground pepper

Per serving:
P: 7 g, F: 17 g, C: 11 g,
kJ: 960, kcal: 229

1 Rinse fresh chicken trimmings under cold water or defrost frozen chicken trimmings according to the instructions on the packet. Prepare the soup vegetables. Peel the celeriac and cut out any bad parts. Peel the carrots and cut off the green leaves and tips. Wash the celeriac and carrots and let them drain. Remove the outer leaves of the leeks, cut off the root ends and dark green leaves. Cut in half lengthways, wash thoroughly and leave to drain. Coarsely chop all the vegetables you have just prepared (photograph 1).

2 Put the soup vegetables in a pan with the water, 1 teaspoon salt, the bay leaf and the allspice. Bring to the boil, skim off the scum (photograph 2), cover and cook for about 40 minutes over medium heat.

3 Meanwhile, peel the carrots, cut off the green leaves and the tips. Peel the kohlrabi. Wash the carrots and kohlrabi and leave to drain. Cut them into cubes or small slices. Top and tail the mangetout peas, wash them and cut the larger ones in half if necessary. Top and tail the green beans and remove any strings there may be. Wash them and cut or break them into small pieces.

4 When the stock is cooked, strain through a sieve and reserve 1 litre/1¾ pints (4½ cups) of the liquid. Bring the liquid to the boil and add the vegetables one after the other. First add the beans, then after about 5 minutes add the carrots and kohlrabi. After a further 5 minutes, add the sugar peas. Cover and cook for a further 5–10 minutes.

5 Rinse the chervil, pat dry, pluck the leaves from the stems and chop finely. Stir the cream into the soup (photograph 3) and season with salt and pepper. Sprinkle with chervil before serving.

Tip: Serve with small semolina dumplings or meatballs.
This soup is suitable for freezing.

Cheese and leek soup

Preparation time:
about 40 minutes;

6 servings

1 kg/2¼ lb leeks
2 tablespoons cooking oil,
e.g. sunflower oil
500 g/18 oz mince (half beef,
half pork)
salt
freshly ground pepper
1 litre /1¾ pints (4½ cups) meat
stock
1 jar sliced mushrooms (drained
weight 300 g/10 oz)
200 g/7 oz cream cheese or
processed cheese, flavoured with
herbs

Per serving:
P: 23 g, F: 29 g, C: 7 g,
kJ: 1577, kcal: 378

1 Remove the outer leaves of the leeks, cut off the root ends and the dark green leaves. Wash the leeks thoroughly and leave to drain. Then cut into thin rings (photograph 1).

2 Heat the oil in a large pan, add the minced beef and pork mixture and fry it in the hot oil. Use a fork or wooden spoon to smooth any lumps that might form (photograph 2) and season with salt and pepper.

3 Add the leeks and brown them lightly for a few minutes. Add the meat stock, bring the mixture to the boil, cover and cook for about 15 minutes over medium heat.

4 Drain the mushrooms in a sieve and add to the soup. Now stir in the cheese (photograph 3) and allow to melt in the hot soup (which must be off the heat). Season the soup with salt and pepper.

Tip: Serve this soup as a light meal with French bread or rolls.

Vegetable noodle soup

Preparation time:
about 75 minutes,
excluding defrosting time;

6 servings

500 g/18 oz fresh or frozen chicken trimmings (pieces of back, neck, wings)
1.25 litres/2¼ pints (5½ cups) water
salt
1.25 kg/2¾ lb vegetables, e.g. carrots, kohlrabi, green beans, cauliflower, broccoli, leeks, courgettes, peas
100 g/3½ oz soup vermicelli
some chicken or vegetable bouillon powder
freshly ground pepper
2 tablespoons chopped parsley

Per serving:
P: 17 g, F: 8 g, C: 17 g,
kJ: 895, kcal: 213

1 Rinse the fresh chicken pieces under cold running water or defrost frozen pieces according to the instructions on the packet. Add the water to a saucepan, add 1 teaspoon salt, add the chicken pieces and bring to the boil, skimming several times. Cover and cook over medium heat for about 40 minutes.

2 Meanwhile, clean the vegetables, wash, leave to drain and slice or dice. Divide the cauliflower and broccoli into florets, then peel and dice the stems.

3 When the cooking time is completed, pour the stock through a sieve and carefully skim off the fat with a spoon. Measure 1.35 litres/2¼ pints (6 cups) stock, making up the quantity with water if necessary. Remove the meat from the bones, take off the skin, cut the meat into small pieces and reserve. Put the stock back into the pot and bring to the boil again.

4 First add the vegetables with longer cooking times, such as the carrots, kohlrabi, green beans and cauliflower. Cover and cook over medium heat for about 8 minutes.

5 Then add the vegetables with shorter cooking times such as the broccoli, courgettes, leeks, peas and the soup vermicelli. Cover and cook everything for a further 5–7 minutes.

6 Season the soup with bouillon powder, salt and pepper. Add the prepared meat and heat it through. Sprinkle with parsley and serve.

Tip: Barely cook the soup vermicelli (follow the instructions on the packet) because they will continue to cook in the hot soup.
If you cook the chicken stock the day before (point 1) and leave it to cool, by the next day the fat will have become solid so that it can be removed with a tablespoon or a skimming spoon.
If you would like more meat in the soup, you can use 4 drumsticks instead of chicken trimmings.

Variation: The vegetable ingredients can be varied according to season. Instead of fresh vegetable you can also use 1 kg/2¼ lb frozen soup vegetables (cooking time according to the instructions on the packaging).

Cream of
vegetable soup (basic recipe)

Preparation times:
about 40 minutes (cream of
pea soup about 30 minutes)

650–1,100 g/1½–2½ lb
vegetables
1 onion
25 g/1 oz (2 tablespoons) butter
or 4 teaspoons cooking oil,
e.g. sunflower or olive oil
1 litre/1¾ pints (4½ cups)
vegetable stock
salt
freshly ground pepper
spices (optional)
croutons, smoked salmon pieces,
sliced leeks, prawns (optional
garnishes)

Per serving
(broccoli variation):
P: 4 g, F: 6 g, C: 4 g,
kJ: 350, kcal: 84

1 Prepare the vegetables and chop up if necessary. Peel and chop the onion. Heat the butter or oil in a pan, add the chopped onion and fry while stirring.

2 Add the prepared vegetables and fry with the onion while stirring. Then add the vegetable stock and bring to the boil. Cook until done.

3 Now purée the soup and season to taste with salt, pepper and appropriate herbs. Add a garnish before serving if desired.

Cream of broccoli soup: Take 700 g/1½ lb broccoli, remove the leaves, separate the florets, peel the stems, cut into pieces and wash both the florets and the stems. Put the stems and florets with the chopped onion in the saucepan. Add the vegetable stock, cover and cook over medium heat for about 8 minutes until done. Now purée the soup. Season with freshly grated nutmeg and if desired add 1–2 teaspoons peeled, grated, roasted almonds or some chopped parsley.

Cream of carrot soup (photograph opposite, bottom right): Take 700 g/1½ lb carrots, peel and cut off the green leaves and tips. Wash the carrots, leave to drain and cut into slices 1 cm/⅜ in thick. Add the carrots to the stock, cover and cook over medium heat for 12 to 15 minutes, then purée. Season the soup with sugar and ground or freshly grated ginger. If desired add 1–2 teaspoons crème fraîche, 1 teaspoon roasted sesame seeds, some chopped dill or even a few strips of smoked salmon in each bowl.

Cream of pumpkin soup: Cut a pumpkin weighing 1.1 kg/2½ lb into segments and peel. Remove the seeds and fibres and cut the flesh into cubes. Add the stock, cover and cook over medium heat for about 15 minutes until done, then purée. Season the soup with sugar and curry or ground ginger. If desired, add 1–2 teaspoons yogurt or crème fraîche, 1–2 teaspoons pumpkin seeds or sesame seeds or chopped dill in each bowl.

Cream of pea soup (photograph opposite, top left): Take 650 g/1½ lb frozen peas, not defrosted. Add the stock, cover and cook over medium heat for about 8 minutes until done, then purée. Season the soup with grated nutmeg, sugar and cayenne pepper. If desired, add 1–2 teaspoons crème fraîche, 1 teaspoon peeled, chopped roasted almonds, some chopped parsley or a few prawns to each bowl.

continued on page 32 ⟹

Cream of potato soup (photograph page 31, top right): Prepare 1 bunch of soup vegetables for the soup. Peel the celeriac and cut out all the bad parts. Peel the carrots, cut off the green leaves and tips. Wash the carrots and celeriac and leave to drain. Remove the outer leaves of the leeks and cut off the root ends and the dark green leaves. Cut in half lengthways, wash thoroughly and leave to drain. Wash, peel and rinse 400 g/14 oz potatoes. Chop all the vegetables you have just prepared. Add the stock, cover and cook over medium heat for about 15–20 minutes, then purée. Season the soup with grated nutmeg. If so desired, add 1–2 teaspoons crème fraîche, some chopped parsley or chopped chervil and a few croutons to each bowl.

Tip: You can also use mixed vegetables (photograph page 31, bottom left).
Vegetable soups should be frozen without their garnish. Just before serving you can add various garnishes to the soup such as croutons, meatballs, 50–75 g/2–3 oz raw or cooked ham cut into strips, 75 g/3 oz smoked salmon cut into strips, or 50–100 g/2–3½ oz prawns.

Unripe spelt grain soup

Preparation time:
about 25 minutes

1 onion
40 g/1½ oz/3 tablespoons butter
100 g/3½ oz (1 cup) spelt flour
generous 1 litre/1¾ pints (4½ cups) vegetable stock
125 ml/4 fl oz (½ cup) whipping cream
salt, pepper, sugar
grated nutmeg
1 tablespoon chopped herbs, e.g. parsley, dill, tarragon, chives

Per serving:
P: 4 g, F: 19 g, C: 20 g,
kJ: 1119, kcal: 267

1 Peel the onion and chop finely. Melt the butter in a saucepan, add the chopped onion and fry until pale yellow, stirring all the while. Add the spelt flour and cook briefly, stirring continuously.

2 Now add the vegetable stock little by little, whisking vigorously and making sure that no lumps are formed. Bring the soup to the boil and cook uncovered over low heat for about 10 minutes, stirring occasionally.

3 Add the cream, heat the soup up again and season with salt, pepper, sugar and nutmeg. Stir in the herbs just before serving.

Tip: Garnish with croutons before serving.

Old German potato soup

Preparation time:
about 90 minutes

For the soup:
700 g/1½ lb floury boiling
potatoes
50–75 g/2–3 oz celeriac
250 g/9 oz carrots
1 onion
1 bay leaf
1 clove
40 g/1½ oz (3 tablespoons)
butter
1.5 litres/2¾ pints (7 cups) hot
vegetable stock
200 g/7 oz leeks
125 ml/4 fl oz (½ cup) whipping
cream or 150 g/5 oz crème
fraîche
salt
freshly ground pepper
dried marjoram leaves
grated nutmeg

For the garnish:
200 g/7 oz chanterelles
1 onion
25 g/1 oz (2 tablespoons) butter
2 tablespoons chopped herbs,
e.g. chervil, chives, flat-leaved
parsley

Per serving:
P: 7 g, F: 24 g, C: 27 g,
kJ: 1483, kcal: 354

1 To make the soup, wash the potatoes, peel and rinse. Peel the celeriac and cut out the bad parts. Peel the carrots, cut off the green leaves and tips. Wash the celeriac and carrots and leave to drain. Cut all these prepared vegetables into small cubes or dice. Peel the onion and stud it with the bay leaf and clove.

2 Melt the butter in a pan. Add the diced celeriac and carrots and brown lightly while stirring all the while. Now add the diced potatoes, studded onion and vegetable stock. Cover, bring to the boil and cook over medium heat for about 20 minutes.

3 Meanwhile, remove the outer leaves of the leeks, cut off the root ends and dark green leaves. Cut in half, wash thoroughly, leave to drain and slice. Add the sliced leeks to the soup, cover and cook for about another 10 minutes.

4 Remove the onion, studded with the bay leaf and clove. Remove about one-third of the potato and vegetable mixture from the soup, purée, stir in the crème fraîche and pour the puréed mixture back into the soup. Heat up the soup again and season with salt, pepper, marjoram and nutmeg.

5 For the garnish: Clean the chanterelles with a brush and remove any bad parts. If necessary, rinse the chanterelles and pat dry. Peel the onion and dice finely. Melt the butter in a pan, add the diced onion and fry in the melted butter, stirring continuously. Add the chanterelles and fry for about 5 minutes, stirring frequently.

6 Add the onion-chanterelle mixture to the soup and simmer for about 5 minutes. Sprinkle with herbs just before serving.

Tip: If desired, small Vienna sausages may also be added to the soup. By preparing the chanterelles while the soup is cooking you can reduce the preparation time by 15 minutes. Bottled or canned chanterelles may be used instead of fresh ones.

Pichelsteiner (meat and vegetable soup)

Preparation time:
about 70 minutes

500 g/18 oz mixed meat from
shoulder or neck (lamb, pork,
beef)
2 onions
30 g/1 oz (2 tablespoons)
clarified butter or margarine
or 2 tablespoons cooking oil,
e.g. sunflower oil
salt
dried marjoram
dried lovage
freshly ground pepper
500 ml/17 fl oz (2¼ cups)
vegetable stock
250 g/9 oz carrots
375 g/13 oz firm potatoes
350 g/12 oz leeks
300 g/10 oz cabbage
2 tablespoons chopped parsley

Per serving:
P: 30 g, F: 17 g, C: 19 g,
kJ: 1469, kcal: 351

1 Rinse the meat under cold running water, pat dry and cut into cubes of 2 cm/¾ in. Peel the onions, cut in half if necessary and slice.

2 Heat the clarified butter, margarine or oil in a pan. Add the cubed meat and brown lightly, stirring continuously (photograph 1). Shortly before the meat has browned sufficiently, add the sliced onions (photograph 2) and fry briefly.

3 Season the meat with salt, marjoram, lovage and pepper. Add the vegetable stock, bring to the boil, cover and cook over medium heat for about 40 minutes.

4 Meanwhile, peel the carrots and cut off the green leaves and tips. Wash the carrots and leave to drain. Wash the potatoes, peel and rinse. Cut both the carrots and potatoes into cubes. Remove the outer leaves of the leeks, cut off the root ends and dark green leaves. Cut in half, wash thoroughly, leave to drain and cut into slices. Remove the dried outer leaves of the white cabbage, cut into quarters, rinse, leave to drain, cut off the base and cut into thin strips (photograph 3).

5 When the meat is done, add the prepared vegetables and potatoes. Bring to the boil, season with salt and pepper, cover and cook for a further 20 minutes.

6 Season with the various herbs and sprinkle with parsley before serving.

Tip: This soup is suitable for freezing.

Soup with green beans

Preparation time:
about 80 minutes

---

500 g/18 oz braising beef,
e.g. from the shoulder
1 onion
2–3 sprigs savory
30 g/1 oz (2 tablespoons)
margarine or clarified butter,
or 2 tablespoons cooking oil,
e.g. sunflower oil
salt
freshly ground pepper
500 ml/17 fl oz (2¼ cups)
vegetable stock
1 kg/2¼ lb green beans
500 g/18 oz firm potatoes
1–2 tablespoons chopped
parsley

Per serving:
P: 33 g, F: 15 g, C: 27 g,
kJ: 1592, kcal: 380

1 Rinse the beef under cold running water, pat dry and cut into cubes of 2 cm/¾ in. Peel and chop the onion. Rinse the savory and pat dry.

2 Heat the margarine, clarified butter or oil in a pan. Add the cubed meat and brown lightly while stirring. Shortly before the meat has browned sufficiently, add the onion and fry briefly.

3 Season the meat with salt and pepper. Add the savory and vegetable stock. Bring to the boil, cover and cook over medium heat for about 40 minutes.

4 Meanwhile, top and tail the green beans removing any strings. Wash the beans and cut or break into small pieces. Wash the potatoes, peel, rinse and cut into pieces.

5 Add the potato and bean pieces and season with salt and pepper. Bring back to the boil, cover and cook for a further 20 minutes.

6 Remove the savory. Season the soup with salt and pepper and sprinkle with parsley before serving.

Tip: This soup is suitable for freezing.

Variation (photograph): A shoulder of lamb may be used instead of beef, and 2–3 tomatoes may also be added. Wash them, leave to drain, make cross-shaped cut, dip briefly in boiling water, then dip them in cold water. Peel the tomatoes, remove the stalks and dice. Add the tomatoes to the soup shortly before the cooking is completed. If desired, sprinkle with basil before serving.

Boiled beef (Tafelspitz)

Preparation time:
about 3 hours

1–1.5 litres/1¾–2¾ pints
(4–4½ cups) water
1 kg/2¼ lb beef (topside)
1–1½ teaspoons salt
1 bay leaf
2 teaspoons peppercorns
2 large onions
150 g/5 oz carrots
150 g/5 oz kohlrabi
150 g/5 oz celeriac
200 g/7 oz leeks

For the horseradish sauce:
30 g/1 oz (2 tablespoons) butter
or margarine
25 g/1 oz (4 tablespoons) plain
(all-purpose) flour
375 ml/12 fl oz (1½ cups) beef
stock
125 ml/4 fl oz (½ cup) whipping
cream
20 g/¾ oz freshly grated
horseradish
salt
a little sugar
about 1 teaspoon lemon juice

1 tablespoon chopped parsley

Per serving:
P: 58 g, F: 22 g, C: 12 g,
kJ: 2011, kcal: 480

1 Pour the water into a large saucepan and bring to the boil. Rinse the beef under cold running water and add to the boiling water. Add the bay leaf and season with salt and peppercorns. Bring to the boil again, cover and simmer very gently for about 2 hours (the liquid should not be allowed to bubble but only move very gently).

2 Meanwhile, peel the onions and chop them. Peel the carrots and cut off the green leaves and the tips. Peel the kohlrabi and celeriac and remove any bad bits. Wash all the vegetables, leave to dry and cut into slices. Remove the outer leaves of the leeks, cut off the root ends and dark leaves. Cut in half lengthways, wash thoroughly and leave to drain and cut into 2 cm/¾ in long pieces.

3 When the meat has cooked, add the prepared vegetables, cover and cook for another 20 minutes.

4 Let the cooked meat rest with the lid on for about 10 minutes so that the meat juices are well distributed. Strain the stock with the vegetables through a sieve, keep the stock and put aside 375 ml/12 fl oz (1½ cups) for the sauce. Cover the vegetables and keep in a warm place.

5 While the meat is resting, melt the butter or margarine for the horseradish sauce in a small pan. Stir in the flour and cook until the mixture turns light yellow, stirring continuously. Add the reserved stock and cream and stir vigorously with a whisk, making sure that there are no lumps. Bring the sauce to the boil, stirring continuously, then simmer uncovered over low heat for about 5 minutes, stirring now and again.

6 Stir in the horseradish. Season the sauce with salt, sugar and lemon juice. Slice the meat and arrange on a preheated dish, pour a little hot stock over it and garnish with the vegetables and parsley. Serve the sauce with the boiled beef.

Tip: Instead of fresh horseradish you can use bottled horseradish sauce. Boiled fillet of beef can be frozen in the stock.
Accompaniment: Potatoes sprinkled with parsley and green salad.

Beef olives (Rouladen)

Preparation time:
about 75 minutes

4 slices beef topside,
180–200 g/7 oz each
salt
freshly ground pepper
medium mustard
60 g/2 oz streaky bacon
4 onions
2 medium-sized pickled gherkins
1 bunch soup vegetables
2 tablespoons cooking oil,
e.g. sunflower oil
about 250 ml/8 fl oz (1 cup) hot
water or vegetable stock
20 g/¾ oz (3 tablespoons) plain
(all-purpose) flour
2 tablespoons water

In addition:
cocktail sticks or kitchen string

Per serving:
P: 42 g, F: 32 g, C: 9 g,
kJ: 2072, kcal: 495

1 Pat the slices of beef dry with kitchen paper, sprinkle with salt and pepper and spread with 2–3 teaspoons of mustard. Cut the bacon into strips. Peel 2 onions, halve and cut into slices. Cut the pickled gherkins into strips.

2 Put the prepared ingredients on the slices of meat. Roll up the slices lengthwise and secure with cocktail sticks or tie with kitchen string.

3 Peel and quarter the remaining 2 onions. Prepare the soup vegetables. Peel the celeriac and cut out any bad parts. Peel the carrots and cut off the green leaves and tips. Wash the celeriac and carrots and let them drain. Remove the outer leaves of the leeks, cut off the root ends and dark green leaves. Cut in half lengthways, wash thoroughly and leave to drain. Cut the prepared ingredients into small pieces.

4 Heat the oil in a saucepan or pan. Brown the beef olives well on all sides. Fry the onions and soup vegetables briefly, then add half the hot water or stock and the beef olives. Braise covered on medium heat for about 1½ hours.

5 While braising, turn the beef olives from time to time and periodically replace the evaporated liquid with hot water or stock. When the beef olives are cooked, remove the cocktail sticks or string, place on a preheated plate and keep warm.

6 Strain the cooking juices through a sieve, make up to 375 ml/ 12 fl oz (1½ cups) water or stock and bring to the boil. Mix the flour with water and stir into the cooking liquid with a whisk, taking care to prevent any lumps from forming. Bring the sauce to the boil and cook uncovered over low heat for about 5 minutes, stirring occasionally. Season the sauce to taste with salt, pepper and mustard.

Accompaniment: Cauliflower, red cabbage (page 98) or peas (page 88) and carrots and boiled potatoes (page 114).

Tip: If desired, you can replace about 100 ml/3½ fl oz (½ cup) of the water or vegetable stock with red wine.

Sauerbraten

(braised beef marinated in vinegar and herbs)

Preparation time:
about 3 hours,
excluding marinating

750 g/1½ lb beef (such as topside, without bones)

For the marinade:
2 onions
1 bunch soup vegetables
5 juniper berries
15 peppercorns
5 allspice berries
2 cloves
1 bay leaf
250 ml/8 fl oz (1 cup) wine vinegar
375 ml/12 fl oz (1½ cups) water or red wine

30 g/1 oz (2 tablespoons) clarified butter, coconut oil or cooking oil, e.g. sunflower oil
salt
freshly ground pepper
375 ml/12 fl oz (1½ cups) marinade liquid
50 g/2 oz honey cake
some sugar

Per serving:
P: 41 g, F: 16 g, C: 14 g,
kJ: 1641, kcal: 392

1 Rinse the beef under cold running water and pat dry.

2 For the marinade, peel the onions and cut into slices. Prepare the green vegetables: Peel the celeriac and remove any bad bits. Peel the carrots and cut off the green leaves and tips. Wash the celeriac and carrots and leave to drain. Remove the outer leaves of the leeks, cut off the root ends and dark leaves. Cut in half lengthways, wash thoroughly and leave to drain. Finely chop all three vegetables.

3 Mix together the onions and green vegetables with the juniper berries, peppercorns, allspice berries, cloves, the bay leaf, wine vinegar and water or red wine in a bowl. Add the meat to the marinade, cover with a lid and leave in the refrigerator for about 4 days, stirring the meat from time to time.

4 Remove the marinated meat from the marinade and pat dry. Pour the marinade through a sieve, reserve 375 ml/12 fl oz (1½ cups) and put the marinade and vegetables to one side.

5 Heat the clarified butter, coconut oil or cooking oil in a pan or casserole. Add the meat, brown well on all sides and season with salt and pepper. Add the drained vegetables and brown briefly with the meat. Add some of the reserved marinade liquid to the meat. Cover and braise the meat over medium heat for about 30 minutes, stirring now and again and replacing the evaporated liquid by adding more marinade whenever necessary.

6 Chop the honey cake finely, add to the meat and braise for another 1½ hours as described above.

7 Let the cooked meat rest for about 10 minutes with the lid on so that the meat juices are well distributed. Slice the meat and arrange the slices on a preheated dish.

8 Rub the braising residue together with the vegetables through a sieve, heat up again, season with salt, pepper and sugar and serve as sauce with the meat.

Accompaniment: Macaroni or potato dumplings (page 120), red cabbage (page 98) and apple sauce or dried fruit. Soak 200 g/7 oz dried fruit in 500 ml/17 fl oz (2¼ cups) apple juice, cover and cook for about 30 minutes. Season with a little salt.

Saxony
onion stew

Preparation time:
about 75 minutes

500 g/18 oz onions
800 g/1¾ lb beef from the neck
about 600 ml/20 fl oz (2½ cups)
water or vegetable stock
salt
freshly ground pepper
½–1 teaspoon caraway seeds
1 bay leaf
about 350 g/12 oz cucumbers
125 g/4½ oz pumpernickel
1–2 teaspoons chopped parsley
(optional)

Per serving:
P: 41 g, F: 16 g, C: 19 g,
kJ: 1621, kcal: 387

1 Peel the onions, cut into quarters and slice. Rinse the beef under cold running water, pat dry and cut into cubes of about 2 cm/¾ in (photograph 1), removing the skin and fat as you do so.

2 Pour the water, seasoned with a scant teaspoon of salt, or the vegetable stock into a large pan and bring to the boil. Add the sliced onion, cubed meat, pepper, caraway and bay leaf, bring the boil, cover and cook over medium heat for about 50 minutes.

3 Meanwhile, peel the cucumber, cut off the ends and dice. Chop the pumpernickel into fine crumbs.

4 Add the pumpernickel (photograph 2) and diced cucumber (photograph 3), season with salt and pepper, cover and cook for a further 10 minutes.

5 Adjust the seasoning with salt and pepper. Sprinkle with parsley before serving if desired.

Accompaniment: Boiled potatoes or potatoes boiled in their skins (page 114) or German farm bread.

Züricher Geschnetzeltes

(thin strips of meat cooked in sauce)

Preparation time:
about 30 minutes

600 g/1¼ lb veal, from the leg
2 onions
40 g/1½ oz (3 tablespoons)
butter or 4 tablespoons cooking
oil, e.g. sunflower oil
salt
freshly ground pepper
15 g/½ oz (2 tablespoons) plain
(all-purpose) flour
250 ml/8 fl oz (1 cup) whipping
cream
125 ml/4 fl oz (½ cup) white
wine
some dashes lemon juice
chervil leaves (optional)

Per serving:
P: 33 g, F: 35 g, C: 6 g,
kJ: 2079, kcal: 497

1 Rinse the veal under cold running water, pat dry and cut into thin strips. Peel the onions, cut in half and chop finely.

2 Heat half the clarified butter or oil in a pan. Add half the strips of meat and fry for 2–3 minutes, stirring frequently. Season with salt and pepper and remove from the pan. Then fry the rest of the meat in the remaining fat and remove from the pan.

3 Add the chopped onion to the remaining cooking fat and fry for about 2 minutes, stirring continuously. Sprinkle the flour on top and fry briefly with the onion. Now add the cream and white wine. Bring to the boil, stirring continuously and cook for another few minutes over medium to high heat while stirring.

4 Return the meat to the pan and heat up in the sauce (do not allow it to boil because the meat would become tough). Season the Geschnetzeltes with salt, pepper, sugar and lemon juice and garnish with chervil leaves if desired.

Accompaniment: Rösti and green salad.

Variation: You can add 250 g/9 oz well cleaned, sliced mushrooms, frying them with the onions (photograph).

Pork escalopes (Schnitzel)

Preparation time:
about 30 minutes

4 escalopes of pork, each about
200 g/7 oz
salt
freshly ground pepper
paprika
1 egg
20 g/¾ oz (3 tablespoons) plain
(all-purpose) flour
40 g/1½ oz (⅜ cup)
breadcrumbs
50 g/2oz (4 tablespoons)
clarified butter, margarine
or 3 tablespoons cooking oil,
e.g. sunflower oil

Per serving:
P: 46 g, F: 15 g, C: 6 g,
kJ: 1450, kcal: 346

1 Rinse the pork under cold running water, pat dry, and sprinkle with salt, pepper and paprika.

2 Beat the egg with a fork in a deep plate. Coat the escalopes first in flour, then in the beaten egg and finally in the breadcrumbs. Press the breadcrumbs firmly onto the chops and shake off any loose crumbs.

3 Heat the clarified butter, margarine or oil in a pan, add the escalopes and fry the escalopes on both sides over medium heat for 8–10 minutes (according to the thickness of the escalopes), turning occasionally. Arrange on a preheated dish.

Accompaniment: Potato chips or boiled potatoes and green salad.

Variation: For Zigeunerschnitzel, prepare the escalopes as in the points above. Add 1 jar (500 g/18 oz) zigeuner sauce to the cooking liquid, heat through and pour over the escalopes.

Cured rib of pork, Kassel style

Preparation time:
about 90 minutes

Cooking time:
about 50 minutes;

6 servings

1.5 kg/3¼ lb Kasseler pork loin
and rib, salted and smoked,
with its bones removed by the
butcher, and chopped
1 onion
1 tomato
1 bunch soup vegetables
1 small bay leaf
125 ml/4 fl oz (½ cup) hot water
sauce thickener (optional)
salt
freshly ground pepper

Per serving:
P: 44 g, F: 16 g, C: 3 g,
kJ: 1390, kcal: 332

1 Wash the meat under cold running water, pat dry and score the fatty skin on top in a criss-cross pattern (photograph 1). Preheat the oven.

2 Peel the onion. Wash the tomatoes, cut into quarters and remove the stalk. Prepare the soup vegetables: peel the celeriac and remove the bad parts, peel the carrots and cut off the green leaves and the tips. Wash the celeriac and carrots and drain. Remove the outer leaves of the leeks, cut off the root ends and dark leaves. Cut in half lengthways, wash thoroughly and leave to drain. Chop all the vegetables finely.

3 Place the meat in a roasting tin rinsed in water, with the fatty skin on top (photograph 2). Add the diced vegetables, bay leaf and bones. Put uncovered in the oven **for about 50 minutes**.

Top/bottom heat: about 200 °C/400 °F (preheated), Fan oven: about 180 °C/350 °F (not preheated), Gas mark 6 (not preheated).

4 When the cooking juices begin to turn brown, add a little hot water (photograph 3). Add more hot water, little by little, as the liquid evaporates and baste the roast with the cooking juices from time to time. Remove the cooked roast and bones from the roasting tin. Cover the meat and leave it to rest for about 10 minutes so that the meat juices are well distributed throughout the roast. Then slice the meat and arrange on a preheated dish.

5 To make the sauce: Loosen cooking deposits stuck to the bottom of the roasting tin with a little water and rub them and the vegetables through a sieve. Pour back into the roasting tin and bring back to the boil. Thicken the sauce with sauce thickener if desired and bring back to the boil briefly. Season the sauce with salt and pepper and serve with the meat.

Accompaniment: Boiled potatoes or potato purée (page 118) and sauerkraut (page 94).

Tip: You may also add 1–2 tablespoons of crème fraîche to the sauce.

Knuckle of pork

Preparation time:
about 3½ hours

Cooking time:
about 2¾ hours;

6 servings

4 salted pork knuckles, each
about 800 g/1¾ lb, with bones
freshly ground pepper
250 ml/8 fl oz (1 cup) hot water
for the fat-collecting roasting tin
about 1 litre/1¾ pints (4½ cups)
hot water, or half vegetable
stock and half water
3 onions
100 ml/3½ fl oz (½ cup) light
beer
dark sauce thickener (optional)

Per serving:
P: 78 g, F: 34 g, C: 1 g,
kJ: 2616, kcal: 622

1 Preheat the oven. Rinse the meat under cold running water, pat dry and rub with pepper. Slide a fat-collecting roasting tin onto the third shelf from the bottom and pour 250 ml/8 fl oz (1 cup) of water into it. Place the knuckles on a grid and slide this grid into the oven above the fat-collecting roasting tin **for about 2¼ hours**.

Top/bottom heat: about 180 °C/350 °F (preheated), Fan oven: about 160 °C/325 °F (not preheated), Gas mark 4 (not preheated).

2 Add hot water or vegetable stock now and again to replace the evaporated liquid (the fat-collecting roasting tin should always be filled with liquid to a height of 1 cm/⅜ in). Turn the meat occasionally and baste with the cooking juices.

3 Peel the onions, cut into quarters and add to the liquid in the fat-collecting roasting tin, then **cook for another 60 minutes at the temperature indicated above**. Baste the knuckle with the beer from time to time.

4 Remove the cooked meat from the bone and arrange on a pre-heated dish.

5 Skim the fat off the cooking juices with a spoon, put aside 500 ml/17 fl oz (2¼ cups) of the cooking juices and top up if necessary with water or stock. Thicken with sauce thickener if desired and season with pepper. Serve the sauce with the meat.

Accompaniment: Sauerkraut (page 94) or white cabbage salad and potato purée (page 118), potato dumplings (page 120) or farm-baked bread.

Tip: You can make the sauce spicier by adding a little mustard. This will also make the sauce more digestible.
The knuckle can also be seasoned with dry marjoram leaves or caraway seeds.
If you prefer the rind crisper, raise the oven temperature by 20–40 °C/70–100 °F for the last 15 minutes.
No more than six knuckles should be cooked in the oven at the same time.

Chicken fricassée

Preparation time:
about 1¾ hours,
excluding cooling time

1.5 litres/2¾ pints (7 cups) water
1 bunch soup vegetables
1 onion
1 bay leaf
1 clove
1 oven-ready chickens 1–1.2 kg/
2¼–2½ lb
1½ teaspoons salt

For the sauce:
25 g/1 oz (2 tablespoons) butter
30 g/1 oz (¼ cup) plain (all-purpose) flour
500 ml/17 fl oz (2¼ cups) chicken stock
1 can asparagus pieces, drained weight 175 g/6 oz
1 tin mushrooms, drained weight 150 g/5 oz
3 tablespoons white wine
about 1 tablespoon lemon juice
1 teaspoon sugar
2 egg yolks from medium eggs
3 tablespoons whipping cream
salt
freshly ground pepper
Worcestershire sauce

Per serving:
P: 41 g, F: 24 g, C: 8 g,
kJ: 1788, kcal: 427

1 Bring the water to the boil in a large saucepan. Meanwhile, prepare the soup vegetables: Peel the celeriac and remove any bad parts. Peel the carrots and cut off the green leaves and the tips. Wash the carrots and celeriac and leave to drain. Remove the outer leaves of the leeks, cut off the root ends and dark leaves. Cut in half lengthways, wash thoroughly and leave to drain. Coarsely chop all the vegetables. Peel the onion and stud it with a bay leaf and a clove.

2 Wash the chicken inside and outside under cold running water, put into the boiling water, bring back to the boil and skim.

3 Now put the prepared vegetables into the saucepan with the chicken, cover and cook for about 60 minutes over low heat.

4 Take the chicken out of the stock and allow to cool a little. Strain the stock through a sieve, remove the fat if necessary and reserve 500 ml/17 fl oz (2¼ cups) of the stock to make the sauce. Loosen the meat from the bones, remove the skin and cut the meat into large pieces.

5 To make the sauce, melt the butter in a pan. Stir in the flour and cook until the mixture turns pale yellow, stirring all the time. Add the reserved stock and beat vigorously with a whisk to obtain a smooth mixture without lumps. Bring the sauce to the boil and cook gently for about 5 minutes without a lid, stirring occasionally.

6 Drain the asparagus pieces and mushrooms in a colander and add to the sauce together with the chicken. Bring back to the boil briefly. Add the white wine, 2 teaspoons lemon juice and sugar.

7 Whisk the egg yolk into the cream and fold carefully into the fricassee to thicken, but do not let the sauce boil any more. Season the fricassee with salt, pepper, Worcestershire sauce and lemon juice.

Accompaniment: Rice or noodles and salad.

Tip: Instead of canned or bottled asparagus you can also buy deep-frozen asparagus. Instead of the tinned mushrooms, 150 g/5 oz fresh mushrooms may be used: clean, slice and fry in 1 tablespoon butter before adding to the sauce (photograph).
The rest of the stock can be used to make soup or incorporate in a sauce. The stock can also be frozen.

Stuffed goose

Preparation time:
about 4¾ hours

Cooking time:
about 3½ hours;

8 servings

1 oven-ready goose, 4–4½ kg/
9–10 lb
salt
freshly ground pepper
dried chopped marjoram

For the stuffing:
50 g/2 oz streaky bacon
2 onions
20 g/¾ oz (1½ tablespoons)
butter or margarine
about 8 day-old bread rolls
(300 g)
300 ml/10 fl oz (1¼ cups) milk
4 medium eggs
3 tablespoons chopped parsley
salt
2 apples

hot water
1 bunch soup vegetables
cold water
10 g/⅓ oz (1 tablespoon) plain
(all-purpose) flour

In addition:
kitchen string
or wooden cocktail sticks

Per serving:
P: 62 g, F: 59 g, C: 27 g,
kJ: 3779, kcal: 895

1 Rinse the inside and outside of the goose under cold running water and pat dry. Sprinkle the inside with salt, pepper and marjoram and rub it in. For the stuffing dice the bacon. Peel and finely chop the onions. Heat the butter or margarine in a pan. Fry the diced bacon until crisp. Then add the chopped onion, sweat until transparent and put to the side. Pre-heat the oven top and bottom. Cut the rolls into small dice and put in a bowl. Bring the milk to the boil in a small pan, pour over the diced rolls and stir well. Add the bacon and onion to the mixture, stir well and leave to cool.

2 Stir the egg and parsley into the mixture and season with salt. Wash and peel the apples, cut in half, remove the cores, grate and stir into the mixture. Put the stuffing inside the goose and sew up the opening with kitchen string or secure with wooden cocktail sticks. Rub the outside of the goose with salt, pepper and marjoram. Pour 125 ml/4 fl oz (½ cup) hot water into a fat-catching roasting tin and put it in the bottom third of the oven. Put the goose with the breast downward on a grid, and put it in the oven above the fat-catching roasting tin **for about 45 minutes**. While it is roasting, prick underneath the wings and legs of the goose from time to time so that the fat can drain out.

Top/bottom heat: about 200 °C/400 °F (preheated), Fan oven: about 180 °C/350 °F (not preheated), Gas mark 6 (not preheated).

3 Remove the accumulated fat and **roast the goose for a further 45 minutes**, skimming off the fat at intervals. When the cooking deposits turn brown, add some hot water so that it is about 1 cm/⅜ in deep in the fat-catching roasting tin. Baste the goose now and then with the roasting liquid, replacing the evaporated liquid from time to time with more hot water. Meanwhile, prepare the soup vegetables. Clean the celeriac and carrots, wash and leave to drain. Clean the leaks, cut in half lengthways, wash thoroughly and leave to drain. Cut the prepared vegetables into pieces. Turn the goose, put the prepared soup vegetables into the fat-catching roasting tin and **cook for about another 2 hours**.

4 Stir ½ teaspoon salt into 50 ml/1½ fl oz (3 tablespoons) cold water. About 10 minutes before end of the cooking time, brush it onto the goose and increase the temperature by about 20 °C/70 °F, so that the skin becomes beautifully crisp. Remove the cooked goose from the fat-catching roasting tin, cover and leave to rest for 5–10 minutes.

5 Put the fat-catching roasting tin on the hob. Loosen the cooking deposits by adding some water and bring to the boil. Rub through a sieve,

continued on page 60 ⟼

make up the quantity to 600 ml/21 oz (2½ cups) with water, put in a pan and bring to the boil. Mix the flour with 50 ml/1½ fl oz (3 tablespoons) water and stir it into the cooking liquid with a whisk, being careful to avoid making any lumps. Bring the sauce to the boil and cook gently uncovered over low heat for about 5 minutes, stirring occasionally. Season the sauce to taste with salt, pepper and marjoram. Carve the goose into portions, put on a preheated dish and serve with the sauce.

Chicken legs (photograph left)

Preparation time:
about 55 minutes

Cooking time:
about 45 minutes

4 drumsticks, each about 250 g/9 oz
½ teaspoon salt
1 pinch freshly ground pepper
1 teaspoon paprika
1–2 tablespoons cooking oil, e.g. sunflower oil

Per serving:
P: 34 g, F: 21 g, C: 0 g,
kJ: 1369, kcal: 327

1 Preheat the oven. Rinse the chicken legs under cold running water, pat dry, cut off any bits of the back that may still be attached and remove any remaining fat and skin.

2 Stir the salt, pepper and paprika into the oil. Rub this mixture on the chicken legs and place in a roasting tin. Put the roasting tin on the middle shelf in the oven **for about 45 minutes**.

Top/bottom heat: about 200 °C/400 °F (preheated), Fan oven: about 180 °C/350 °F (preheated), Gas mark 6 (preheated).

Variation 1: Tandoori chicken legs (photograph bottom right)
Stir 125 g/4½ oz natural yogurt (3.5% fat) until smooth. Peel 1 clove of garlic, press through a garlic press and stir into the yogurt. Add ½ teaspoon salt, 1–1½ teaspoons sweet paprika, ½–1 teaspoon Madras curry, a scant ½ tea-spoon ground cinnamon, a small pinch of cayenne pepper and a pinch of ground cloves; stir well. Prepare the chicken legs as described in point 1 and rub them with this marinade, put in a shallow dish, cover and leave for at least 2 hours or overnight in the refrigerator. Now put the chicken legs in a roasting tin as described above, coat again with the marinade and roast as indicated above. If you like you can baste the chicken legs again with the marinade half-way through the roasting process and sprinkle them with sesame seeds.

Variation 2: Chicken legs with a herb crust (photograph top right). Prepare the chicken legs as described in point 1 and rub with salt, pepper and sweet paprika. Mix together 4–5 tablespoons chopped mixed herbs (fresh or deep-frozen, e.g. parsley, tarragon, chives) with 6 tablespoons breadcrumbs. Now coat the chicken first in flour, then in 1 beaten egg and finally in the breadcrumbs, pressing to ensure that the breadcrumbs stick to the chicken legs. Put the chicken legs in a roasting tin as described above, sprinkle them with 3–4 tablespoons vegetable oil (e.g. sunflower oil) and roast as indicated above.

Saddle of venison, Baden style

Preparation time:
about 90 minutes

Cooking time:
35–50 minutes

1 saddle of venison with bones,
weighing about 1.6 kg/3½ lb
salt
freshly ground pepper
75 g/3 oz sliced streaky bacon
1 onion
50 g/2 oz celeriac
100 g/3½ oz carrots
5 juniper berries
125 ml/4 fl oz (½ cup) dry red
wine or vegetable stock
2–3 pears, e.g. Williams
Christian
200 ml/7 fl oz (⅞ cup) sweet
white wine
juice of 1 lemon
200 ml/7 fl oz (⅞ cup) dry red
wine
250 ml/8 fl oz (1 cup) whipping
cream
180 g/6½ oz cranberry preserve
dark sauce thickener (optional)

Per serving:
P: 67 g, F: 31 g, C: 29 g,
kJ: 2925, kcal: 699

1 Preheat the oven. Rinse the saddle of venison under cold running water, pat dry and remove the skin (photograph 1). Rub the meat with salt and pepper and place it in a casserole rinsed in water, and cover with slices of bacon.

2 Peel and finely chop the onions. Clean the celeriac and carrots, peel, wash, leave to drain and dice. Place the casserole without lid in the oven **for 35–50 minutes**. As soon as the juices begin to brown, add the juniper berries and red wine or vegetable stock.

Top/bottom heat: about 200 °C/400 °F (preheated), Fan oven: about 180 °C/350 °F (not preheated), Gas mark 6 (not preheated).

3 Meanwhile, wash the pears, cut in half and remove the core, preferably with a scoop-shaped melon baller (photograph 2). Add the pear halves to the white wine and lemon juice, bring to the boil and cook over medium heat for about 10 minutes. Take the pears out of the liquid with a skimming ladle and leave to cool.

4 Take the cooked meat out of the roasting tin, cover and let rest for about 10 minutes. Deglaze the cooking juices with red wine and strain with the vegetables through a sieve, bring to the boil and stir in the cream. Add 2 tablespoons cranberry sauce, bring back to the boil and allow to bubble for 3–5 minutes. You can add the meat juices which have run out of the resting meat to the sauce. Thicken the sauce with gravy thickener if you like, and season again with the various condiments.

5 Remove the slices of bacon. Loosen the meat from the bone, cut into slices and put back on the bone (photograph 3) and arrange on a preheated dish.

6 Fill the pear halves with the rest of the cranberry sauce and place around the saddle. Serve the sauce separately.

Accompaniment: Spätzle (page 126), mushrooms and red cabbage (page 98).

Haunch of venison

Preparation time:
about 3 hours, excluding
marinating time

Cooking time:
2–2½ hours;

6 servings

1.5 kg/3¼ lb haunch of venison
with bones
2 tablespoons cooking oil,
e.g. sunflower oil
1 teaspoon each dried marjoram
and thyme
1 teaspoon dried rosemary
100 g/3½ oz thinly sliced fatty
bacon
salt
freshly ground pepper
about 150 ml/5 fl oz (⅝ cup) hot
game or vegetable stock
1 onion
100 g/3½ oz carrots
150 g/5 oz leeks

For the sauce:
125 ml/4 fl oz (½ cup) red wine
250 ml/8 fl oz (1 cup) game
or vegetable stock
100 ml/3½ fl oz (½ cup)
whipping cream
20 g/¾ oz (3 tablespoons) plain
(all-purpose) flour
2 tablespoons cold water
2 tablespoons cranberries (from
the jar)
some small thyme leaves

Per serving:
P: 46 g, F: 19 g, C: 6 g,
kJ: 1640, kcal: 392

1 Rinse the meat under cold running water, pat dry and remove the skin. Stir the marjoram, thyme and rosemary into the oil and coat the haunch with this mixture. Cover and leave in the refrigerator overnight.

2 Preheat the oven. Arrange half the bacon slices in a roasting pan, pre-rinsed with water. Sprinkle salt and pepper over the venison, place it on top of the bacon slices in the roasting pan and cover with the rest of the bacon slices. Put the roasting pan without lid in the oven for **about 60 minutes**.

Top/bottom heat: about 200 °C/400 °F (preheated), Fan oven: about 180 °C/350 °F (not preheated), Gas mark 6 (not preheated).

3 As soon as the cooking juices begin to brown add 150 ml/5 fl oz (⅝ cup) hot game or vegetable stock. Baste the meat from time to time with the cooking juices and replace the evaporated liquid with hot water or hot stock whenever necessary.

4 Meanwhile, peel the onions. Peel the carrots and cut off the green leaves and the tips. Remove the outer leaves of the leeks, cut off the root ends and dark leaves. Cut in half lengthways, wash thoroughly and leave to drain. Coarsely chop all the vegetables. After the 60 minutes roasting time, add the vegetables to the roasting pan with meat and **cook for a further 60–90 minutes**.

5 Allow the cooked venison to rest covered for about 10 minutes to ensure that the meat juices are well distributed. Remove the slices of bacon, cut into slices and arrange on a preheated dish.

6 To make the sauce, deglaze the cooking juices with red wine and game or vegetable stock. Strain this liquid with the vegetables through a sieve, add the cream and bring back to the boil. Mix flour and water together and stir well to obtain a smooth consistency. Add to the boiling liquid, stirring continuously to make sure that no lumps are formed. Simmer gently without a lid for about 5 minutes, stirring occasionally. Add the cranberries, thyme and if you like the meat juices that have run out from the meat while it was resting. Season the sauce and serve with the meat.

Accompaniment: Boiled potatoes (page 114) or potato dumplings (page 120) and red cabbage (page 98) or Brussels sprouts (page 98).

Venison ragout

Preparation time:
about 90 minutes

800 g/1¾ lb venison from the leg, boned, e.g. deer, boar
75 g/3 oz streaky bacon
1 onion
30 g/1 oz (2 tablespoons) clarified butter or 2 tablespoons cooking oil, e.g. sunflower oil
salt
freshly ground pepper
10 g/⅓ oz (1½ tablespoons) plain (all-purpose) flour
4 juniper berries
3 cloves
2 pinches dried thyme
250 ml/8 fl oz (1 cup) vegetable stock or game stock
250 g/9 oz mushrooms or chanterelles
4 teaspoons red currant jelly
4 teaspoons port
50 g/2 oz (4 tablespoons) cold butter flakes

Per serving:
P: 47 g, F: 25 g, C: 8 g,
kJ: 1880, kcal: 449

1 Rinse the meat under cold running water, pat dry, remove the skin and cut into cubes of about 2.5 cm/1 in (photograph 1). Finely dice the bacon. Peel and chop the onion.

2 Heat the clarified butter or oil in a pan. Add the diced bacon and fry until golden brown. Now add the cubed meat, brown well on all sides and season with salt and pepper.

3 Add the chopped onion and brown with the meat. Sprinkle flour over the meat. Add a good half of the hot vegetable or game stock to the pan together with the juniper berries, cloves and thyme. Bring to the boil while stirring, then cover and cook the meat over medium heat for about 55 minutes. Replace the evaporated liquid with vegetable or game stock whenever necessary.

4 Meanwhile, cut the stalks off the mushrooms (photograph 2) and remove any bad parts, wipe clean with kitchen paper, rinse if necessary and pat dry (large mushrooms should be halved or quartered). Add the mushrooms to the ragout and cook for another 5 minutes.

5 Stir in the red currant jelly (photograph 3), beat in the butter flakes and season the ragout with salt and pepper.

Accompaniment: Boiled potatoes (page 114), potato dumplings (page 120) or Spätzle (page 126), red cabbage (page 98) or Brussels sprouts (page 98) and cranberry sauce.

Tip: Marinating the meat overnight in buttermilk will make the meat more tender and reduce the strong taste of game. Then pat thoroughly dry and cut into cubes.
The sauce may also be thickened with dark gravy thickener instead of butter.

Pheasant with sauerkraut and wine

Preparation time:
about 1¾ hours

Cooking time:
about 65 minutes

1 onion
1 can sauerkraut, drained weight
770 g/1¾ lb
1 small bay leaf
a few peppercorns
a few juniper berries
salt
250 ml/8 fl oz (1 cup) white
wine
1 oven-ready pheasant of about
1 kg/2¼ lb
6 slices streaky bacon
200 g/7 oz black grapes
200 g/7 oz white grapes
some sugar

chervil or parsley
tomato segments

Per serving:
P: 58 g, F: 16 g, C: 19 g,
kJ: 2108, kcal: 503

1 Preheat the oven, top and bottom. Peel and chop the onion, then mix it well with the sauerkraut, bay leaf, peppercorns and juniper berries. Season with salt, put in an ovenproof dish or casserole and pour the wine over it.

2 Rinse the pheasant inside and out under cold running water, wipe dry, cut into quarters and rub with salt inside and out. Position it on the sauerkraut so that as much as possible is covered by the pheasant. Arrange the bacon slices over the pheasant. Cover the soufflé dish or roasting pan and put in the oven **for about 25 minutes**.

Top/bottom heat: about 200 °C/400 °F (preheated), Fan oven: about 180 °C/350 °F (not preheated), Gas mark 6 (not preheated).

3 At this point, remove the lid and **cook for a further 30 minutes at the same oven temperature**.

4 Meanwhile, wash the grapes, drain, cut in half and remove the pips.

5 Remove the cooked pheasant pieces from the ovenproof dish or casserole, cover and let rest for 10 minutes.

6 Add the grapes to the sauerkraut, mix well and season with sugar. Cover the ovenproof dish or casserole with a lid and return to the oven. **Cook for about another 10 minutes at the same oven temperature.**

7 Arrange the pheasant pieces on the sauerkraut on a preheated dish and garnish with chervil or parsley and tomato segments.

Accompaniment: Potato purée (page 118).

Tip: Instead of pheasant you can also use partridge.

Truite à la meunière (photograph)

Preparation time:
about 20 minutes

4 prepared trout, 200 g/7 oz
each, salt, pepper
40 g/1½ oz (6 tablespoons)
plain (all-purpose) flour
2 tablespoons cooking oil,
e.g. sunflower oil
40 g/1½ oz (3 tablespoons)
butter
lemon slices (untreated)

Per serving:
P: 31 g, F: 8 g, C: 4 g,
kJ: 929, kcal: 222

1 Rinse the trout under cold running water, pat dry and rub with salt inside and out. Coat in flour and shake off any excess.

2 Heat the oil in a pan, add the trout and brown on both sides over medium heat. Add the butter and melt. Fry the trout for about 10 minutes, turning them over frequently.

3 Garnish the trout with lemon slices before serving.

Accompaniment: Boiled potatoes sprinkled with parsley (page 114), mixed green salad (page 104).

Variation: Trout with almonds (photograph): add 50–75 g (2–3 oz) slivered almonds and brown in the pan with the trout. Sprinkle over before serving.

Salmon trout with leaf spinach

Preparation time:
about 80 minutes,
excluding oven cooking time

Cooking time: about
35 minutes (small trout),
about 55 minutes (large trout);

6 servings

1.5 kg/3¼ lb leaf spinach
200 g/7 oz shallots
2 cloves of garlic
300 g/10 oz mushrooms
150 g/5 oz tomatoes
4 teaspoons butter or margarine
salt, freshly ground pepper
grated nutmeg
1 large salmon trout, 1.3 kg/
2¾ lb, or 2 small salmon trout,
each about 600 g/1¼ lb
75 g/3 oz smoked, streaky
bacon
1 bunch parsley
1 lemon (untreated)
6 thin slices streaky bacon

Per serving:
P: 48 g, F: 10 g, C: 5 g,
kJ: 1311, kcal: 312

1 Remove any yellow, wilted leaves of the spinach including the thick stems. Wash carefully in plenty of water and leave to drain. Peel the shallots and cloves of garlic. Cut half the shallots into eighths and finely chop the rest with the cloves of garlic. Wipe the mushrooms clean with kitchen paper, slice off the base of the stalks or remove entirely if they are tough and woody. If necessary rinse and pat dry. Slice half the mushrooms and chop up the rest finely. Wash the tomatoes, wipe dry, remove the stalks, cut into quarters and dice.

2 Melt the butter or margarine in pan. Add the shallots, cut into eighths, the garlic and sliced mushrooms and braise briefly. Add the spinach and braise briefly, but sufficiently to make it "collapse". Season with salt, pepper and nutmeg. Stir the diced tomatoes into the spinach.

3 Preheat the oven. Rinse the sea trout under cold running water inside and out, then pat dry. Rub with salt both inside and out. Chop the bacon finely. Rinse the parsley, pat dry, remove the leaves from the stalks and chop finely. Wash the lemon in hot water, grate the zest, cut the lemon in half and squeeze. Mix together the diced bacon, chopped mushrooms and shallots, parsley, grated lemon zest and juice and stuff this mixture inside the abdominal cavity of the trout.

continued on page 72 ➡

4 Arrange the spinach in a large rectangular soufflé dish or roasting pan. Place the stuffed trout on top and perhaps garnish with remaining stuffing. Arrange the slices of bacon on the trout and put the soufflé or roasting pan in the oven on the third shelf from the bottom **for about 35 minutes (small trout) or 55 minutes (large trout).**

Top/bottom heat: about 200 °C/400 °F (preheated), Fan oven: about 180 °C/350 °F (preheated), Gas mark 6 (preheated).

Accompaniment: Boiled potatoes (page 114) or rice.

Plaice with bacon

Preparation time:
about 30 minutes

4 prepared plaice, about 300 g/
10 oz each
salt
freshly ground pepper
40 g/1½ oz (6 tablespoons)
plain (all-purpose) flour
about 150 g/5 oz lean, streaky
bacon
2–3 tablespoons cooking oil,
e.g. sunflower oil
lemon segments
some sprigs of dill

Per serving:
P: 36 g, F: 9 g, C: 6 g,
kJ: 1039, kcal: 248

1 Rinse the plaice under cold running water, pat dry, rub with salt and pepper and coat in flour (photograph 1). Dice the bacon. Heat the oil in a large pan and fry the diced bacon so that the fat runs out (photograph 2). Then remove from the pan and keep in a warm place.

2 Depending on the size of the pan, brown the plaice on both sides in the bacon fat for about 15 minutes, one after the other (photograph 3). Add a little more fat if necessary. Arrange the plaice on a preheated dish and keep warm until all the plaice are cooked.

3 Sprinkle the diced bacon over the plaice and garnish with the lemon segments and sprigs of dill.

Accompaniment: Boiled potatoes (page 114) and lamb's lettuce.

Tip: You can also brown 150–200 g/6–7 oz crabmeat in the bacon fat and sprinkle over the plaice with the bacon.

Herring fillets, home-made style (photograph)

Preparation time:
about 30 minutes,
excluding marinating time

8 pickled herring fillets (Matjes, about 600 g/1¼ lb)
250 ml/8 fl oz (1 cup) water, salt
3 onions
400 g/14 oz apples
150 g/5 oz pickled gherkins (from the jar)
375 ml/12 fl oz (1½ cups) whipping cream
2 tablespoons lemon juice
salt, pepper, some sugar

Per serving:
P: 30 g, F: 53 g, C: 15 g,
kJ: 2767, kcal: 660

1 Rinse the herring fillets under cold running water, pat dry, remove any bones that may still remain and cut the fillets in cubes of 2 cm/¾ in.

2 Bring water to the boil in a pan. Add some salt. Peel the onions, cut in half, slice and blanch briefly in the boiling salted water, then leave to drain.

3 Wash the apples, peel, cut into quarters and remove the cores. Drain the pickled gherkins. Slice the apples and pickled gherkins.

4 Mix the lemon juice and cream together, season with salt, pepper and sugar, and stir in the sliced onions, apples and pickled gherkins. Put the herring fillets in the sauce, cover and leave in the refrigerator for about 12 hours to marinate.

Accompaniment: Boiled potatoes and fried onion rings, green beans with bacon (page 88) or fried potatoes.

Smoked fish mousse

Preparation time:
about 15 minutes,
excluding cooling time

2 smoked trout fillets, about 125 g/4½ oz each
30 g/1 oz (2 tablespoons) soft butter
2–4 teaspoons sour cream
1–1¼ teaspoons lemon juice
salt
freshly ground pepper
some lamb's lettuce
½ teaspoon pink pepper berries

Per serving:
P: 14 g, F: 9 g, C: 0 g,
kJ: 591, kcal: 141

1 Chop the trout fillets coarsely, remove any bones that may be left and purée the fillets with butter, sour cream and lemon juice.

2 Season the mixture with salt and pepper and refrigerate for about 60 minutes.

3 Cut off the root ends of the lamb's lettuce in such a way that the leaves still hold together. Remove yellowing, wilted leaves, wash the lettuce thoroughly, spin dry and arrange on 4 plates.

4 Shape the smoked fish mousse into balls using 2 tablespoons, dipped in hot water, and arrange on the lamb's lettuce salad. Garnish with pink pepper berries before serving.

Accompaniment: Ciabatta (Italian white bread), wholewheat bread or black bread.

Tip: The smoked fish mousse can also be served as a starter.

Marinated salmon

Preparation time:
about 25 minutes,
excluding marinating time;

8 servings

1 kg/2¼ lb fresh salmon
3 bunches dill
40 g/1½ oz salt
30 g/1 oz (2 tablespoons) sugar

For the dill sauce:
1 bunch dill
2 tablespoons strong mustard
2 tablespoons medium mustard
3 rounded tablespoons sugar
2 tablespoons white wine vinegar
3 tablespoons cooking oil, e.g. sunflower oil

Per serving:
P: 24 g, F: 15 g, C: 12 g,
kJ: 1144, kcal: 274

1 Rinse the salmon under cold running water, pat dry, cut in half lengthways and remove the bones, using tweezers if necessary (photograph 1).

2 Rinse the dill, pat dry, pull the leaves off the stems and chop finely. Mix the salt and sugar together and sprinkle on the two salmon halves, then sprinkle the chopped dill on top.

3 Place one salmon half with the skin downwards in a large shallow dish that is larger than the fish and a chopping board that will weigh it down. Put the other salmon half on top with the skin facing upward and cover with clingfilm. Put a small chopping board (which should be larger than the fish) on top and weigh it down with 2 or 3 weights or full, unopened cans (photograph 2). Keep the salmon refrigerated for 2–3 days, turning it periodically two or three times and basting it with the marinade.

4 Cut the salmon into thin slices at an angle towards the skin side (photograph 3) and arrange on a dish.

5 For the dill sauce, rinse the dill under cold running water, pat dry, pull the leaves off the stems and chop finely. Stir the two kinds of mustard, sugar and vinegar together and little by little whisk in the oil. Stir in the dill and serve the sauce with the salmon.

Accompaniment: Black bread or farm-baked bread with butter.

Tip: Before marinating the salmon, sprinkle with 1–2 tablespoons crushed white peppercorns and/or 1 tablespoon crushed juniper berries.

Variation: For marinated salmon trout, rinse 1 prepared salmon trout (about 1 kg/2¼ lb) under cold running water, pat dry and cut in half lengthways. Remove the backbone and the rest of the bones. Then follow the instructions above from stage 2 onwards.

Mussels cooked in wine

Preparation time:
about 60 minutes

2 kg/4½ lb mussels
2 onions
1 bunch soup vegetables
50 g/2 oz (4 tablespoons) butter
or margarine
500 ml/17 fl oz (2¼ cups) dry
white wine
salt
freshly ground pepper

Per serving:
P: 10 g, F: 12 g, C: 2 g,
kJ: 1027, kcal: 245

1 Wash the mussels thoroughly in plenty of cold water and brush each one individually (photograph 1) until they no longer feel sandy (any mussels that open while being washed are not edible). Remove filaments if there are any (photograph 2).

2 Peel the onions and cut in rings. Prepare the soup vegetables: peel the celeriac and remove the bad parts, peel the carrots and cut off the green leaves and the tips. Wash the celeriac and carrots and leave to drain: Remove the outer leaves of the leeks, cut off the root ends and dark leaves. Cut in half lengthways, wash thoroughly and leave to drain. Coarsely chop the vegetables.

3 Melt the butter or margarine in a pan. Add the onions and soup vegetables and fry briefly while stirring. Add the white wine, season with salt and pepper and bring to the boil. Put the mussels in, cover and heat them without boiling until they open up (about 10 minutes) stirring occasionally. (Any mussels that have not opened during cooking are not edible).

4 Remove the mussels from the cooking liquid with a skimming ladle (photograph 3) and put in a preheated bowl. Strain the cooking liquid through a sieve, season with salt and pepper and serve with the mussels.

Accompaniment: Wholemeal bread with butter.

Variation: For mussels Livorno style (main photograph), prepare the mussels as indicated in point 1. Peel 6 tomatoes and chop into cubes. Peel 2 onions and chop finely. Peel 2 cloves of garlic and push through a garlic press. Finely chop 2 preserved chillies. Heat 8 tablespoons olive oil in a large pan. Add the onions, garlic and chillies and braise, stirring continuously. Add the chopped tomatoes and 200 ml/7 fl oz (⅞ cup) vegetables stock or white wine and bring to the boil. Add the mussels and braise for about 10 minutes, stirring now and again. Season with salt and pepper and garnish with lemon quarters before serving.

Frankfurt green sauce (photograph)

Preparation time:
about 30 minutes

about 150 g/5 oz fresh herbs for
Frankfurt green sauce
150 g/5 oz crème fraîche or sour
cream
1 small onion
150 g/5 oz natural yogurt
3–4 teaspoons olive oil
1 teaspoon mustard
1 squeeze lemon juice
½ teaspoon sugar
salt, white pepper

Per serving:
P: 4 g, F: 15 g, C: 7 g,
kJ: 736, kcal: 176

1 Rinse the herbs, pat dry, remove the leaves from the stems, chop coarsely and purée with 2 tablespoons crème fraîche or sour cream. Or simply chop the herbs very finely. Peel the onion and chop finely.

2 Now stir the herbs and cream mixture or the finely chopped herbs into the rest of the crème fraîche or soured cream together with the yogurt, chopped onion, oil and mustard. Season the sauce with lemon juice, sugar, salt and pepper and refrigerate until serving.

Uses: Frankfurt green sauce can be served with new potatoes, with hard-boiled eggs or with boiled beef.

Tip: The "real" Frankfurt sauce includes 7 fresh herbs, but the herbs can be varied according to the season. You can also buy bunches of mixed herbs, specially put together for Frankfurt green sauce, each about 150 g/5 oz. If these are not available where you live, you can also buy a large bunch of mixed herbs, for instance, parsley, chives, chervil, burnet, borage, lemon balm, cress or sorrel. If you cannot find fresh herbs you can also use deep-frozen herbs (4 packs of 25 g/1 oz each).

Cheese sauce

Preparation time:
about 15 minutes

30 g/1 oz (2 tablespoons) butter
or margarine
25 g/1 oz (4 tablespoons) flour
375 ml/12 fl oz (1½ cups)
vegetable stock
150 g/5 oz soft cheese
salt
a few squeezes of lemon juice

Per serving:
P: 6 g, F: 18 g, C: 5 g,
kJ: 845, kcal: 202

1 Melt the butter or margarine in a saucepan. Add the flour and stir until the mixture turns pale yellow.

2 Add the vegetable stock and stir vigorously with a whisk, making sure that there are no lumps.

3 Bring the sauce to the boil and simmer gently for 5 minutes without a lid, stirring occasionally.

4 Add the soft cheese and stir to make it melt in the sauce. Season with salt and lemon juice.

Uses: Cheese sauce is delicious served with Brussels sprouts (page 98), or with meat such as medallions of pork.

Tip: To reduce the calories you can use half of the cheese and replace the other half with herb or paprika quark. The sauce should not be allowed to boil after the quark has been added.

continued on page 82 ⮕

Variation: To make a blue cheese sauce, use only 10 g/1⅓ oz flour, replace the processed cheese with 150 g/5 oz Roquefort or gorgonzola and add 5 tablespoons whipping cream. Season the sauce with 1–2 tablespoons white wine instead of lemon juice and a little pepper. Serve with noodles.

Mushroom sauce

Preparation time:
about 20 minutes

250 g/9 oz mushrooms
50 g/2 oz streaky bacon
2 teaspoons cooking oil,
e.g. sunflower oil
250 ml/8 fl oz (1 cup) vegetable stock
15 g/½ oz (1 tablespoon) soft butter
15 g/½ oz (2 tablespoons) plain (all-purpose) flour
150 g/5 oz crème fraîche
salt
freshly ground pepper
2 teaspoons chopped parsley

Per serving:
P: 6 g, F: 18 g, C: 5 g,
kJ: 846, kcal: 204

1 Remove stalk ends of the mushrooms, cut out any bad parts and wipe clean with kitchen paper. Rinse if necessary, pat dry and slice. Dice the bacon.

2 Heat the oil in a pan. Add the diced bacon and braise briefly, stirring continuously. Now add the sliced mushrooms and the stock and bring to the boil and simmer gently uncovered for about 5 minutes.

3 Knead the butter and flour together, add to the mixture and stir with a whisk or mixing spoon to dissolve it in the sauce. Let the sauce simmer gently uncovered for about 5 minutes, stirring occasionally.

4 Stir in the crème fraîche. Season the sauce with salt and pepper and stir in the parsley.

Uses: Mushroom sauce is delicious served with beef steak, schnitzel and fried fish fillets or steak.

Variation 1: To make a vegetarian mushroom sauce, leave out the bacon and braise the mushrooms in 15 g/½ oz (1 tablespoon) butter or 1–2 table- spoons olive oil. In addition, season the sauce with 1 tea-spoon chopped rosemary.

Variation 2: For a mushroom sauce with ceps, rinse about 10 g/⅓ oz dried ceps in a sieve under cold water and allow to drain. Heat up the vegetable stock, remove from the heat, add the ceps and leave to soak for about 30 minutes. Prepare the sauce as indicated above and add the stock with the ceps.

Mayonnaise (photograph bottom right)

Preparation time:
about 10 minutes

1 yolk of 1 medium egg
1–2 teaspoons white wine
vinegar or lemon juice
salt
½–1 teaspoon medium mustard
125 ml/4 fl oz (½ cup) cooking
oil, e.g. sunflower oil

Per serving:
P: 1 g, F: 33 g, C: 0 g,
kJ: 1231, kcal: 294

1 Whisk together the egg yolk with the vinegar or lemon juice, salt and mustard in a bowl, using a whisk or hand-mixer with a whisk attachment to obtain a thick mixture.

2 Add the oil little by little, 1–2 tablespoons at a time, stirring continuously (with this method it is not necessary to dribble the oil in drop by drop because the spices added to the egg yolk will prevent the mayonnaise from curdling).

Uses: Mayonnaise is an ideal base for cold sauces and dips, and is delicious served with a fondue or in sandwiches.

Tip: All the ingredients used to make the mayonnaise should be the same temperature so that they bind together properly.
Should the mayonnaise curdle, mix together 1 egg yolk and vinegar or lemon juice and stir the mayonnaise into it little by little.

Note: Only use very fresh eggs; check the sell-by date! Store the mayonnaise in the refrigerator and consume within 24 hours.

Variation 1: For a light mayonnaise (top of photograph), make the mayonnaise as described above but use only 5 tablespoons oil. Then add 4 tablespoons low-fat quark and 1 tablespoon whipping cream to the mayonnaise. Optionally, ½ peeled, crushed clove of garlic may be added.

Variation 2: To make a cold curry sauce (bottom left of photograph), make the mayonnaise as described above, add 1–2 teaspoons curry powder and 150 g/5 oz natural yogurt (3.5% fat) or sour milk. To make a sweet curry sauce, add 1–2 tablespoons of apricot jam, rubbed through a sieve, to the curried mayonnaise described here.

Variation 3: To make a remoulade sauce (centre right of photograph), shell 2 hard-boiled eggs, rub the egg yolks through a sieve and chop up the egg whites. Mix the hard-boiled egg yolk with 1 raw egg yolk and make the mayonnaise as described above. Finally add 1 medium-sized, finely chopped pickled gherkin, 2 tablespoons chopped herbs (for instance, parsley, chives, dill, chervil or cress), 1 teaspoon drained, chopped capers and stir in the chopped egg white. Season the remoulade sauce with salt, pepper and sugar.

Variation 4: To make tartare sauce (centre left of photograph) peel 4 shallots or small onions, chop finely and add to the mayonnaise together with 2 teaspoons drained, chopped capers, 2 tablespoons chopped herbs (such as parsley, dill or chervil). Season with salt.

Parsnip and carrot medley (photograph)

Preparation time:
about 25 minutes

300 g/10 oz carrots
700 g/1½ lb parsnips
50 g/2 oz (4 tablespoons) butter
125 ml/4 fl oz (½ cup) vegetable stock
salt
freshly ground pepper
2 teaspoons cut smooth parsley

Per serving:
P: 2 g, F: 11 g, C: 19 g,
kJ: 782, kcal: 187

1 Peel the carrots and parsnips and cut off the green leaves and tips. Wash and leave to drain. Cut the carrots into thin slices. Cut the tops of the parsnips into thin slices, quarter the lower ends and cut into thin slices lengthways.

2 Melt the butter in a saucepan. Cook the carrot slices over low heat for about 5 minutes while stirring. Add the sliced parsnips and vegetable stock. Add salt and pepper and cook the vegetables covered for a further 6–8 minutes, stirring occasionally.

3 Season the vegetables to taste with salt and pepper, sprinkle with parsley and serve.

Tip: Serve the parsnip and carrot medley with fish dishes, fried poultry and veal or poultry ragouts.

Variation: Parsley and carrot medley with kohlrabi. Use only 400 g/ 14 oz parsnip and in addition 300 g/10 oz kohlrabi. Prepare the 3 kinds of vegetables as described above, cutting the kohlrabi first into quarters and then into slices. Cook the kohlrabi slices and 1–2 teaspoons of thyme together with the carrot slices and proceed as described above.

Kohlrabi

Preparation time:
about 30 minutes

1 kg/2¼ lb kohlrabi
30 g/1 oz (2 tablespoons) butter
100 ml/3½ fl oz (½ cup) vegetable stock
salt
grated nutmeg
2 teaspoons chopped parsley

Per serving:
P: 3 g, F: 7 g, C: 6 g,
kJ: 410, kcal: 98

1 Peel the kohlrabi, putting aside some of the soft kohlrabi leaves for garnishing the dish. Wash the kohlrabi, leave it to drain and cut it first into slices, then into strips.

2 Melt the butter in a pan. Gently cook the kohlrabi strips while stirring. Add the vegetable stock. Cook the kohlrabi covered over low heat for 10–15 minutes, stirring occasionally.

3 Season the kohlrabi with salt and nutmeg. Rinse the kohlrabi leaves that have been put aside, leave to drain and chop. Sprinkle the kohlrabi with the green leaves and parsley before serving.

Tip: Serve kohlrabi with meat or poultry dishes, or as part of an assorted vegetable dish.

Green beans (photograph)

1 Bring water to the boil in a saucepan. Meanwhile, cut the ends off the beans and pull off any strings. Wash the beans and cut or break into pieces. Rinse the savory. Add salt to the cooking water at the rate of 1 teaspoon per 1 litre/1¾ pints (4½ cups) water. Add the beans and savory, bring to the boil again and cook the beans covered for 15–20 minutes.

2 In the meantime, peel and dice the onion. Melt the butter or margarine. Lightly braise the diced onion.

3 Drain the cooked beans in a colander and remove the savory. Add the beans to the diced onion and stir. Season the beans with salt, pepper and nutmeg, sprinkle with parsley and serve.

Tip: Green beans can be part of a dish of assorted vegetables (photograph). They can be served with meat dishes, or with herrings. Yellow wax beans can be prepared in the same way. Princess or Kenya beans are very tender, with a cooking time of 8–12 minutes. Dip the cooked beans in cold water so that they keep their green colour.

Variation: Green beans with bacon. Put 70 g/3 oz diced streaky bacon in a pan, add butter or margarine and sweat gently. Add the diced onion and lightly braise. Add the beans and toss together. Serve with lamb.

Preparation time:
about 30 minutes

750 g/1½ lb green beans
3–4 sprigs savory
salt
1 onion
40 g/1½ oz butter or margarine
freshly ground pepper
grated nutmeg
2 teaspoons chopped parsley

Per serving:
P: 4 g, F: 9 g, C: 10 g,
kJ: 570, kcal: 136

Petit pois (peas)

1 Melt the butter in a pan. Add the peas without defrosting and cook gently while stirring. Add salt, sugar and the vegetable stock, then cook covered over low heat for about 8 minutes, stirring occasionally.

2 Season the peas with salt and sugar, sprinkle with parsley and serve.

Tip: Serve the peas with meat or poultry dishes, or as part of an assorted vegetable dish (photograph).
If using fresh peas, 2 kg/4½ lb unshelled peas in their pods are needed to make 750 g/1½ lb peas. Shell the peas, wash, leave to drain and then cook as described above.

Preparation time:
about 15 minutes

35 g/1¼ oz butter
750 g/1½ lb frozen petit pois (peas)
salt, 1 pinch sugar
100 ml/3½ fl oz (½ cup) vegetable stock
2 teaspoons chopped parsley

Per serving:
P: 14 g, F: 8 g, C: 24 g,
kJ: 965, kcal: 230

Stuffed peppers

Preparation time:
about 80 minutes,
excluding cooling time

4 peppers, 150 g/5 oz each
250 g/9 oz large onions
500 g/18 oz tomatoes
4 tablespoons olive oil
400 g/14 oz minced meat,
half beef, half pork
4 teaspoons tomato purée
salt
freshly ground pepper
about 375 ml/12 fl oz (1½ cups)
vegetable stock
15 g/½ oz (2 tablespoons) plain
(all-purpose) flour
4 tablespoons whipping cream
salt
freshly ground pepper
dried chopped oregano
some sugar

Per serving:
P: 23 g, F: 37 g, C: 14 g,
kJ: 1992, kcal: 475

1 Wash the peppers and dry them. Cut off and reserve the stalk end of each pepper to make a "lid". Remove the seeds as well as the white pith inside and rinse the peppers. Peel and chop the onions. Wash the tomatoes, dry and remove the stalks. Cut 3 tomatoes in half, remove the cores and dice.

2 Heat two tablespoons of oil in a pan. Gently cook half the chopped onions in it. Add the minced meat and brown while stirring, breaking up any lumps with a fork.

3 Mix in the diced tomatoes and half the tomato purée, season with salt and pepper and leave to cool. Then fill the prepared peppers with the mixture. Put the "lid" back on each pepper.

4 Cut the remaining tomatoes into pieces. Heat the remaining oil in a large saucepan. Add the remaining chopped onions and cook gently. Put the peppers next to each other in the pan. Add the tomato pieces and 375 ml/12 fl oz (1½ cups) vegetable stock. Cook the peppers covered over low heat for about 50 minutes. Then put the peppers on a preheated dish.

5 For the sauce, pour the cooking liquid with the tomato pieces and onions through a sieve. Measure off 375 ml/12 fl oz (1½ cups), adding vegetable stock to make up the quantity if necessary. Stir in the remaining tomato purée and bring all to the boil. Mix the flour with the cream and stir into the cooking liquid little by little. Cook gently for about 10 minutes, stirring occasionally.

6 Season the sauce with salt, pepper, oregano and sugar and serve with the stuffed peppers.

Accompaniment: Rice, boiled potatoes or potatoes boiled in their skins, and a mixed green salad (page 104).

Variation: Peppers stuffed with chicken or turkey. Replace the minced meat with 400 g/14 oz chopped chicken or turkey breast fillets. Rinse the fillets under running cold water, pat dry, cut into very fine dice (or cut into large dice and purée with the slicing attachment of the hand mixer). Then continue as described above. Season the sauce with 2 tablespoons chopped parsley instead of oregano.

Celeriac escalopes (photograph)

Preparation time:
about 25 minutes,
excluding frying time

800 g/1¾ lb celeriac
salt
freshly ground pepper
4 teaspoons lemon juice
2 eggs
100 g/3½ oz (1 cup) plain (all-purpose) flour
200 g/7 oz breadcrumbs
3 tablespoons cooking oil,
e.g. sunflower oil
50 g/2 oz (4 tablespoons) butter

Per serving:
P: 8 g, F: 21 g, C: 31 g,
kJ: 1439, kcal: 344

1 Peel the celeriac, cut out any bad parts, wash and leave to drain. Cut into slices 5 mm/3⁄16 in thick and sprinkle with salt, pepper and lemon juice.

2 Whisk the eggs in a deep plate with a fork. Dip the celeriac slices first in flour, then in the egg and finally in the breadcrumbs. Press the breadcrumbs firmly onto the slices.

3 Heat some of the oil in a frying pan. Fry the celeriac slices a few at a time for about 4 minutes per side until golden yellow. Shortly before the end of the cooking time of each batch add some butter to the pan and melt it.

Tip: Serve the celeriac as a vegetarian entrée, e.g. with tomato sauce, herb curd cheese and salad.
Slices of radish may be served, or prepare cut red beet in slices.

Variation: The celeriac can also be made with different coatings. For these, mix 180 g/6½ oz breadcrumbs with 30 g/1 oz grated Parmesan cheese or 30 g/1 oz finely chopped sunflower seeds.

Shallots in red wine

Preparation time:
about 30 minutes

500 g/18 oz shallots
25 g/1 oz (2 tablespoons) butter
20 g/¾ oz sugar
250 ml/8 fl oz (1 cup) red wine
salt
freshly ground pepper
2 teaspoons chopped smooth parsley

Per serving:
P: 2 g, F: 5 g, C: 10 g,
kJ: 562, kcal: 134

1 Peel the shallots and halve if necessary. Melt the butter and cook the shallots in it until golden yellow. Scatter the sugar over top and stir until it caramelises.

2 Add the red wine and cook shallots uncovered over low heat for about 15 minutes. Season the shallots with salt and pepper to taste and sprinkle with parsley before serving.

Tip: Serve the shallots with steaks, fried liver or roasts.
Instead of butter, the shallots can be cooked in 3 tablespoons of olive oil.
The shallots in red wine will keep for about 1 week in the refrigerator. Served cold, they taste good on bread, or they may be part of an appetiser plate.

Variation: Stir 100 g/3½ oz crème fraîche into the cooked shallots and season again to taste.

Hunter's cabbage (photograph)

Preparation time:
about 45 minutes

1 kg/2¼ lb cabbage
1 small onion
100 g/3½ oz streaky bacon
4 teaspoons cooking oil,
e.g. sunflower oil
250 ml/8 fl oz (1 cup) vegetable
stock
salt
freshly ground pepper
herb vinegar
1 pinch sugar

Per serving:
P: 7 g, F: 7 g, C: 9 g,
kJ: 560, kcal: 134

1 Remove the outer wilted leaves from the cabbage, cut the cabbage into quarters, rinse, leave to dry, cut out the stalk and cut the cabbage into fine strips. Peel and chop the onion. Cut the bacon into dice.

2 Heat the oil in a pan and add the diced bacon. Then add the chopped onion and cook gently while stirring. Then add the cabbage strips and continue cooking gently, stirring from time to time.

3 Add the vegetable stock, season the cabbage with salt and pepper and cook covered over low heat for about 25 minutes. Season to taste with salt, pepper, vinegar and sugar.

Tip: Hunter's cabbage is an excellent accompaniment for braised pork with boiled potatoes.
Instead of ordinary cabbage, hunter's cabbage may be made with Savoy cabbage, pointed cabbage or Chinese cabbage. With pointed or Chinese cabbage, reduce the cooking time to 10–15 minutes.

Sauerkraut

Preparation time:
about 60 minutes

4 onions
1 apple
2 tablespoons cooking oil,
e.g. sunflower oil
750 g/1½ lb sauerkraut
125 ml/4 fl oz (½ cup) water
or white wine
1 bay leaf
4 juniper berries
6 peppercorns
salt, sugar, pepper

Per serving:
P: 3 g, F: 8 g, C: 7 g,
kJ: 514, kcal: 123

1 Peel and chop the onions. Wash the apple, peel, quarter, core and cut into slices.

2 Heat the oil in a pan. Gently cook the chopped onion. Pull the sauerkraut loosely apart and add the water or white wine. Put the apple slices on the sauerkraut.

3 Add the bay leaf, juniper berries and peppercorns, season with salt and cook the sauerkraut covered over low heat for 25–30 minutes, stirring occasionally. Add some liquid at intervals if necessary. Season the sauerkraut with salt, sugar and pepper.

Tip: Serve the sauerkraut with cured rib of pork Kassel style (page 52) and potato purée (page 118).
Sauerkraut becomes thicker if a grated raw potato is added in the last 10 minutes of cooking.
If desired, replace the apple with 150 g/5 oz pineapple pieces (from the can, drained from the juice). Add some pineapple juice to the sauerkraut to taste.

Cabbage beef olives

Preparation time:
about 90 minutes

salt
1 head Savoy or white cabbage, about 1.5 kg/3¼ lb
1 day-old roll
1 onion
1 medium egg
about 1 teaspoon medium mustard
375 g/13 oz minced beef
freshly ground pepper
3 tablespoons cooking oil, e.g. sunflower oil
250 ml/8 fl oz (1 cup) vegetable stock
20 g/¾ oz (3 tablespoons) plain (all-purpose) flour
4 teaspoons cold water

In addition:
kitchen string or cocktail sticks

Per serving:
P: 25 g, F: 25 g, C: 13 g,
kJ: 1570, kcal: 375

1 Bring plenty of water to the boil in a large saucepan. Add salt at the rate of 1 teaspoon salt per 1 litre/1¾ pints (4½ cups) water. Meanwhile, remove the outer wilted leaves from the Savoy or white cabbage, rinse the cabbage and cut out a wedge shape from the stalk. Cook the cabbage in the boiling salted water until the outer leaves come off. Repeat this process until you have about 12 large leaves that are fairly soft. Let the leaves drain, pat dry with kitchen paper and cut off the fat leaf-ribs.

2 For the filling, soak the roll in cold water. Peel and chop the onion. Squeeze the water firmly from the roll, then mix the roll with the chopped onion, egg and mustard. Season the mixture with salt and pepper.

3 For each olive put 2–3 large cabbage leaves on top of each other and put part of the filling on it. Turn up the leaves at the sides and roll them up. Secure the wrapped beef olives with kitchen string or with cocktail sticks.

4 Heat the oil in a pan. Brown the beef olives on all sides. Add the vegetable stock and cook the beef olives covered over low heat for about 45 minutes, turning them occasionally.

5 When the beef olives are done, remove the kitchen string or cocktail sticks and put them on a preheated plate.

6 Stir the flour and water together. Bring the cooking liquid to the boil, stir in the flour mixture with a whisk, bring to the boil again and cook gently for about 5 minutes. Season the sauce to taste with salt and pepper and serve with the beef olives.

Accompaniment: Boiled potatoes (page 114), potato purée (page 118), breadcrumb dumplings (page 130) or potato dumplings (page 120).

Tip: Use the remaining cabbage for Savoy cabbage, hunter's cabbage (page 94), or for a soup or a stew.

Variation 1: Add 1–2 teaspoons of curry powder to the filling and season the sauce strongly with curry powder and cayenne pepper.

Variation 2: Instead of the day-old roll, mix 50 g/2 oz cooked rice with the chopped meat.

Brussels sprouts (photograph)

Preparation time:
about 30 minutes

1 kg/2¼ lb Brussels sprouts
salt
40 g/1½ oz butter
grated nutmeg

Per serving:
P: 9 g, F: 9 g, C: 6 g,
kJ: 607, kcal: 145

1 Bring some water to the boil in a saucepan. Remove any damaged outer leaves from the Brussels sprouts, cut the ends off the stalks, cut a cross in the stalk ends, wash and leave to drain.

2 Add the Brussels sprouts and salt at the rate of 1 teaspoon salt to 1 litre/1¾ pints (4½ cups) cooking water, bring to the boil and cook covered over low heat for about 15 minutes.

3 When they are done, put the Brussels sprouts in a colander and leave to drain. Melt the butter, toss the Brussels sprouts in it and season with salt and nutmeg.

Tip: Serve Brussels sprouts with roast meat such as game, pork or goose.
If using frozen Brussels sprouts, 800–900 g/1¾–2 lb are needed for 4 servings. Cook the frozen sprouts as described above.

Red cabbage

Preparation time:
about 75 minutes

1 kg/2¼ lb red cabbage
375 g/13 oz sharp apples,
e.g. Cox
2 onions
50 g/2 oz lard or 3 tablespoons
cooking oil
1 bay leaf
3 cloves
3 juniper berries
5 allspice berries
salt, pepper, sugar
4 teaspoons red wine vinegar
2 tablespoons red currant jelly
125 ml/4 fl oz (½ cup) water

Per serving:
P: 3 g, F: 13 g, C: 24 g,
kJ: 953, kcal: 228

1 Remove the outer wilted leaves from the red cabbage, rinse the cabbage, cut into quarters, rinse, leave to drain and cut out the stalk. Slice the cabbage very finely. Wash the apples, peel, cut in quarters, remove the cores and cut into small pieces. Peel and chop the onions.

2 Heat the lard or oil in a pan. Gently cook the diced onion while stirring. Add the sliced cabbage and apple pieces, then continue cooking gently.

3 Add the bay leaf, cloves, juniper berries, allspice berries, salt, peppers, sugar, vinegar, red currant jelly and water. Cook the red cabbage covered over low heat for 45–60 minutes, stirring occasionally. Season the red cabbage to taste with salt and sugar.

Tip: It is a good idea to prepare red cabbage in larger quantities and freeze it divided into servings. Red cabbage should still have some "bite", so it should not be overcooked.
Instead of water, red cabbage can be cooked in the same quantity of red or white wine, and the red currant jelly can be replaced with 2 tablespoons stewed cranberries.

Ceps (photograph)

1 Cut the stalks off the ceps and remove any bad parts, wipe clean with kitchen paper, rinse if necessary, pat dry and cut into slices lengthways. Peel and finely chop the garlic. Cut out the stalks from the tomatoes, peel and dice.

2 Heat half the oil in a pan. Cook half the sliced ceps over medium heat for 5–7 minutes. Season with salt and pepper, remove, put on preheated plates and keep in a warm place. Cook the remaining sliced ceps in the same way.

3 Sweat the garlic in the remaining cooking oil. Add the diced tomato and heat through. Stir in the parsley. Season with salt and pepper and pour over the ceps.

Preparation time:
about 30 minutes

500 g / 18 oz ceps
1 clove garlic
150 g / 5 oz tomatoes
3 tablespoons olive oil
salt
freshly ground pepper
2 teaspoons chopped parsley

Per serving:
P: 6 g, F: 13 g, C: 2 g,
kJ: 576, kcal: 137

Mushroom in cream sauce

1 Cut the stalks off the mushrooms and remove any bad parts, wipe clean with kitchen paper, rinse if necessary and pat dry. Cut the mushrooms into slices or the oyster mushrooms into strips. Peel and chop the onion. Cut off the root ends from the spring onions, remove the dark green parts, wash the spring onions, leave to drain and cut into rings.

2 Heat the butter in a wide pan. Gently cook the chopped onion while stirring. Add the mushrooms and cook them gently as well. Add the vegetable stock and the mushrooms. Cook covered over low heat for 6–8 minutes, stirring occasionally. Season with salt and pepper.

3 Add the spring onion rings and cook for 1–2 minutes. Stir in the crème fraîche and heat through. Season to taste with cayenne pepper, Worcestershire sauce, lemon juice and sugar and sprinkle with parsley.

Tip: Serve mushrooms in cream-sauce with steaks, escalopes or breadcrumb dumplings (page 130).
White wine may be used instead of vegetable stock.

Preparation time:
about 35 minutes

800 g / 1¾ lb mushrooms
or oyster mushrooms
2 onions
1 bunch spring onions
30 g / 1 oz (2 tablespoons) butter
salt, pepper
100 ml / 3½ fl oz (½ cup) vegetable stock
150 g / 5 oz crème fraîche
1 pinch cayenne pepper
Worcestershire sauce
about 1 teaspoon lemon juice
some sugar
4 teaspoons chopped flat-leaved parsley

Per serving:
P: 9 g, F: 18 g, C: 8 g,
kJ: 937, kcal: 226

Rocket with
Parmesan (photograph)

Preparation time:
about 25 minutes,
excluding cooling time

30 g/1 oz pine kernels
125 g/4½ oz rocket
200 g/7 oz cocktail tomatoes
30 g/1 oz Parmesan

For the sauce:
1–2 tablespoons balsamic
vinegar
½ teaspoon liquid honey
salt, pepper
3 tablespoons olive oil

Per serving:
P: 6 g, F: 19 g, C: 3 g,
kJ: 852, kcal: 203

1 Fry the pine nuts in a pan without fat until golden-brown and leave to cool.

2 Sort the rocket and remove all the yellowing, wilted leaves. Cut off the thicker stems, wash the rocket, spin dry and cut the larger leaves in half. Wash the cocktail tomatoes, dry and cut in half or quarters. Grate the Parmesan.

3 To make the sauce, mix together the vinegar and honey, season with salt and pepper and whisk in the oil. Arrange the rocket in a dish and garnish with cocktail tomatoes. Drizzle the dressing over it and sprinkle the pine nuts and Parmesan on top.

Tip: This salad is ideal as a starter or with grilled dishes or fried meat. Instead of pine nuts you can use peeled, flaked almonds or coarsely chopped walnuts.

Chinese cabbage
with fromage frais

Preparation time:
about 25 minutes

600 g/1¼ lb Chinese cabbage
1 can tangerines, drained weight
175 g/6 oz
100 g/3½ oz cooked ham

For the sauce:
100 g/3½ oz fresh herb cheese
3 tablespoons each whipping
cream and tangerine juice, from
the can
3–4 teaspoons vinegar
salt, sugar, pepper
2 teaspoons assorted, chopped
herbs, e.g. basil, parsley, chives

Per serving:
P: 10 g, F: 9 g, C: 12 g,
kJ: 723, kcal: 173

1 Remove the outer, wilted leaves of the Chinese cabbage and cut in half. Remove the hard inner stalk, rinse, drain thoroughly and cut in narrow strips.

2 Drain the tangerines in a sieve, reserve the juice and put 4 tablespoons aside. Cut the ham into strips.

3 To make the sauce, mix together the fromage frais, cream and tangerine juice and season with vinegar, salt, sugar and pepper. Stir in the herbs. Put all salad ingredients in a bowl and stir in the dressing just before serving.

Tip: This salad can also be served as a light meal with bread or rice. It also makes an ideal party salad, but in this case the salad and the dressing should be served separately. You can also use iceberg lettuce instead of Chinese cabbage.

Mixed green salad

Preparation time:
about 20 minutes

¼ head Lollo Rossa or Lollo Bionda
¼ head oak leaf salad
200 g/7 oz chicory

For the sauce:
1 small onion
1–2 tablespoons herb vinegar
salt
1 pinch sugar
crushed, dried green peppercorns
4 tablespoons olive oil
2 teaspoons chopped herbs, e.g. parsley, chive, chervil

Per serving:
P: 1 g, F: 15 g, C: 3 g,
kJ: 635, kcal: 152

1 Remove the outer, yellowing leaves of the two kinds of lettuce. Wash, spin dry and tear into smaller pieces (photograph 1).

2 Remove the outer, wilted leaves of the chicory, cut in half lengthways, wash, leave to drain and cut out the bitter, wedge-shaped inner stalks (photograph 2). Cut the chicory into strips and mix together in a bowl with the two kinds of lettuce.

3 To make the sauce, peel the onion and chop finely. Mix together the vinegar, salt, sugar and peppercorns. Whisk in the oil and stir in the chopped onion and herbs (photograph 3). Pour the dressing over the salad, mix carefully and serve immediately.

Tip: This mixed green salad can be served as a starter and is also delicious served with meat and fish dishes, pasta and gratins.
Store fresh green salad in a large plastic bag, fill it with a little air and close carefully. Place the bag in the vegetable compartment where the lettuce cannot be crushed and will remain fresh for longer because of the air inside the bag.

Variation 1: The possibilities for variations on this recipe are endless. For instance, you can replace the round lettuce with curly endive, fresh spinach or lamb's lettuce, use hazelnut or walnut oil instead of olive oil, and raspberry vinegar instead of herb vinegar.

Variation 2: For a mixed green salad with escalopes, rinse 500 g/18 oz chicken, turkey or pork escalope under cold running water, pat dry, cut into thick slices and marinate in a mixture of 3 tablespoons soya sauce, seasoned with pepper. Then drain the meat slices and fry on both sides in 3 tablespoons of hot oil (for instance, sunflower oil) for about 4–6 minutes. Arrange the slices of meat, hot or cold, on the salad and serve immediately.

Carrot and apple salad (photograph)

Preparation time:
about 20 minutes

500 g/18 oz carrots
250 g/9 oz slightly sharp apples,
e.g. Elstar, Cox

For the sauce:
2 tablespoons lemon juice
1–2 teaspoons sugar or honey
salt
1 teaspoon cooking oil,
e.g. sunflower oil

Per serving:
P: 1 g, F: 1 g, C: 13 g,
kJ: 296, kcal: 71

1 Peel the carrots and cut off the green leaves and tips, wash and leave to drain. Wash the apples, peel, cut into quarters and remove the cores. Grate the carrots and the apples.

2 To make the lemon sauce, mix together the lemon juice, sugar or honey and salt and whisk in the oil. Pour the sauce over the grated carrots and apples and mix well. Adjust the seasoning by adding salt and sugar to taste.

Tip: If the apples are untreated you can simply wash them, dry them and grate them with the skin on.
You can also add a pinch of ground ginger to the sauce.

Green bean salad

Preparation time:
about 35 minutes,
excluding soaking time

750 g/1½ lb green beans
3–4 branches savory
250 ml/8 fl oz (1 cup) water
¼ teaspoon salt

For the sauce:
1 onion
1–2 tablespoons vinegar,
e.g. herb vinegar
salt, pepper, some sugar
2 tablespoons cooking oil,
e.g. sunflower or olive oil
2 teaspoons chopped herbs,
e.g. parsley, dill, savory

Per serving:
P: 4 g, F: 8 g, C: 10 g,
kJ: 547, kcal: 130

1 Top and tail the beans, remove any strings, wash and cut or break into pieces and rinse the savory. Bring water to the boil in a pan and add salt. Add the green beans and savory to the salted boiling water, bring back to the boil, cover and cook over medium heat for 15–20 minutes.

2 Drain the cooked beans in a colander, rinse briefly in cold water and leave to drain. Remove the savory.

3 To make the sauce, peel the onion and chop finely. Mix together the vinegar, salt, pepper and sugar and whisk in the oil. Add the chopped onion and herbs and mix well. Pour the dressing over the green beans while they are still warm, mix well and let it soak in.

4 Season the salad again with salt, pepper and sugar just before serving.

Tip: Green bean salad is delicious served with grilled fish, steak or cold roast, or as part of a mixed salad dish.
It is important that the beans are still warm when the dressing is added so that they soak in all the herbs and spices.
If you want to be really quick you can use 2 cans of green beans (drained weight 340 g/12 oz each).

Tomato and onion salad

Preparation time:
about 35 minutes;

4–6 servings

500 ml/17 fl oz (2¼ cups) water
250 g/9 oz onions
2 teaspoons vinegar, e.g. herb vinegar
½ teaspoon salt
500 g/18 oz tomatoes
3 hard-boiled eggs
1 tablespoon chopped parsley leaves
freshly ground pepper

For the mayonnaise:
1 yolk of 1 medium egg
2 teaspoons herb vinegar
1 slightly rounded teaspoon medium sharp mustard
salt
1 teaspoon sugar
freshly ground pepper
125 ml/4 fl oz (½ cup) cooking oil, e.g. sunflower oil
3 tablespoons natural yogurt (3.5% fat)
2 tablespoons chopped herbs, e.g. chives, parsley, oregano

Per serving:
P: 7 g, F: 30 g, C: 6 g,
kJ: 1358, kcal: 324

1 Bring the water to the boil. Meanwhile, peel the onions and cut into slices. Add the vinegar, salt and sliced onions to the boiling water, cover and cook over low heat for about 5 minutes, then leave to drain.

2 Wash the tomatoes, wipe dry and remove the stalks. Shell the eggs. Slice the tomatoes and eggs and arrange them with the sliced onions and parsley in alternate layers in a salad bowl. Sprinkle salt and pepper over the sliced eggs and tomatoes.

3 For the mayonnaise, mix together the egg yolk, vinegar, mustard, salt, sugar and pepper in a mixing bowl and stir with a whisk or hand-held mixer with whisk attachment until it forms a thick mass. Gradually add the oil 1–2 tablespoons at a time, and whisk to incorporate. Stir in the yogurt and herbs. Pour the mayonnaise over the salad ingredients and put the salad in the refrigerator.

Tip: Serve the tomato and onion salad with steak, grills, ham, or as a part of a party buffet.
The onions will have lost their sharpness by being boiled in water seasoned with salt and vinegar. They are therefore more digestible but still have a bite.
Ready-made mayonnaise may also be used for the sauce. Simply stir yogurt and herbs into it.

Note: Use only very fresh eggs for the mayonnaise. Keep the prepared salad in the refrigerator and consume within 24 hours.

Variation 1: If you like, you can use leeks instead of onions. In this case, remove the outer leaves, root ends and dark green leaves and cut in half lengthways. Wash thoroughly, leave to drain and cut into rings. Blanch the leeks for 1 minute in boiling salted water and leave to drain.

Variation 2: To make a quick tomato salad, wash 750 g/1½ lb small, firm tomatoes, wipe dry, remove the stalks and cut into slices. For the sauce, peel 1 small onion, chop up finely, mix together with 2 tablespoons vinegar (for instance white wine or herb vinegar) and season with salt and vinegar. Whisk in 4 tablespoons vegetable oil (e.g. sunflower oil). Pour the sauce over the sliced tomatoes, mix well and let stand briefly.

Pork sausage and cheese salad (photograph)

Preparation time:
about 35 minutes,
excluding soaking time

250 g/9 oz onions
250 g/9 oz Emmental cheese
350 g/12 oz cooked pork sausages
75 g/3 oz pickles

For the sauce:
4 teaspoons wine vinegar
4 teaspoons water
1 teaspoon mustard
salt, pepper, sugar
3 tablespoons cooking oil
2 teaspoons chopped chives

Per serving:
P: 28 g, F: 51 g, C: 4 g,
kJ: 2481, kcal: 539

1 Peel the onions, cut into rings, put in boiling water and cook for 2 minutes. Pour into a sieve and leave to drain. Remove the rind from the Emmental cheese and cut into strips. Remove the skin from the sausage and cut the meat in half lengthways if necessary. Cut the sausage meat and pickled gherkins into slices.

2 To make the sauce, mix together the vinegar with the water, add the mustard, salt, pepper and sugar and whisk in the oil. Pour the dressing over the salad ingredients and mix well. Leave the salad to stand for 1 hour for the sauce to impregnate the ingredients. Sprinkle with chopped chives before serving.

Tip: The pork sausage and cheese salad can be served as a light meal with pretzels or rolls or as part of a party buffet.
This salad can also be prepared with chicken meat sausage.

Variation: To make a smoked loin of pork and cheese salad, use smoked loin of pork instead of pork sausage, cut into strips and add to the salad.

Egg salad with leeks

Preparation time:
about 40 minutes

300 g/10 oz leeks
300 g/10 oz carrots
½ head iceberg lettuce (about 150 g/5 oz)
6 hard-boiled eggs

For the sauce:
100 g/3½ oz salad mayonnaise
150 g/5 oz natural yogurt
4 teaspoons lemon juice
salt, pepper, sugar
2 teaspoons chopped chives

Per serving:
P: 14 g, F: 24 g, C: 9 g,
kJ: 1287, kcal: 307

1 Remove the outer leaves of the leeks, cut off the root ends and dark leaves. Cut in half lengthways, wash thoroughly, leave to drain and cut into very fine strips. Peel the carrots and cut off the green leaves and tips. Wash the carrots, leave to drain and grate coarsely.

2 Remove the outer, yellowing leaves of the iceberg lettuce, cut into very fine strips, wash and spin dry. Shell the eggs and cut into six segments (perhaps with an egg slicer).

3 To make the mayonnaise, mix together the yogurt and lemon juice and season with salt, pepper and sugar. Stir the dressing into the prepared salad ingredients (except for the eggs) and mix well. Check the seasoning and adjust if necessary. Garnish with the egg segments and sprinkle the chopped chives on top.

Tip: Serve the egg and leek salad with bread or boiled potatoes as a light meal. It is also ideal as part of a party buffet.

Potato salad with mayonnaise

Preparation time:
about 45 minutes, excluding
cooling and soaking time

800 g/1¾ lb firm cooking
potatoes, 2 onions
250 ml/8 fl oz (1 cup) vegetable
stock
100 g/3½ oz pickled gherkins
(from the jar)
3 hard-boiled eggs

For the sauce:
3 tablespoons mayonnaise
2 tablespoons gherkin liquid
salt, freshly ground pepper

Per serving:
P: 10 g, F: 10 g, C: 29 g,
kJ: 1044, kcal: 249

1 Wash the potatoes, put in a saucepan filled with water, bring to the boil, cover and cook over medium heat for about 20–25 minutes. Drain the potatoes when cooked, rinse briefly under cold running water and leave to drain. Peel while still hot and leave to cool down. Then cut the potatoes into slices and put in a large bowl.

2 Peel the onions, cut into very small cubes and bring to the boil in the vegetable stock. Cover and cook for 1 minute. Pour the hot onion and stock mixture over the sliced potatoes and leave to soak for at least 30 minutes. Cut the pickled gherkins into slices or cubes. Shell the eggs and cut into cubes.

3 For the sauce, stir the liquid from the gherkins into the mayonnaise. Then mix together all the ingredients with the cooled potato slices in the onion stock mixture. Season with salt and pepper and leave to stand for at least 30 minutes.

Warm potato salad (photograph bottom)

Preparation time:
about 50 minutes,
excluding soaking time

Cooking time: 15–20 minutes

1 kg/2¼ lb firm cooking
potatoes

For the sauce:
2 onions
75 g/3 oz fatty bacon
125 ml/4 fl oz (½ cup) vegetable
stock
2–3 tablespoons herb vinegar
salt
freshly ground pepper
1 pinch sugar

4 teaspoons chopped chives

Per serving:
P: 6 g, F: 15 g, C: 35 g,
kJ: 1263, kcal: 301

1 Wash the potatoes, put in a pan and cover with water. Bring to the boil, cover and cook over low heat for about 20–25 minutes.

2 In the meantime, peel the onions for the sauce and cut into cubes. Dice the bacon, put in a frying pan without fat and cook over medium heat so that the fat is released. Strain the fat through a sieve into a small bowl and reserve the fried diced bacon. Add the diced onions to the stock and bring to the boil. Cover and cook for about 5 minutes. Add the vinegar, salt, pepper and sugar and stir in the bacon fat.

3 Drain the potatoes when cooked and rinse briefly in cold water. Drain again and peel while still hot. Cut into slices and arrange in a heat-resistant dish. Pour the salad dressing over the sliced potatoes and mix well. Leave to stand for a few hours so that the flavours can soak in. Preheat the oven. Check the seasoning and add salt, pepper and vinegar to taste. Put the dish in the oven **for 15–20 minutes** and stir occasionally.

Top/bottom heat: about 150 °C/300 °F (preheated), Fan oven: about 130 °C/250 °F (not preheated), Gas mark ½ (preheated).

4 Stir in the chives, scatter the bacon on top and serve warm.

Potatoes boiled
in their skins (photograph)

Preparation time:
about 30 minutes

about 1 kg/2¼ lb potatoes

Per serving:
P: 5 g, F: 0 g, C: 33 g,
kJ: 670, kcal: 160

1 Thoroughly wash the potatoes, cover with water and bring to the boil, then cook covered for 20–25 minutes.

2 Drain the potatoes, quench with cold water, drain and peel immediately.

Tip: These potatoes can be served as a side dish or with herb curd cheese and salad as an entrée.
The potatoes can be used in a salad or for making sauté potatoes.
A firm potato is preferable for this purpose.

Boiled potatoes

Preparation time:
about 30 minutes

750 g/1½ lb potatoes
1 teaspoon salt

Per serving:
P: 3 g, F: 0 g, C: 22 g,
kJ: 447, kcal: 106

1 Wash the potatoes, thinly peel with a knife or potato peeler and remove any eyes.

2 Rinse the potatoes again, cut the larger potatoes into two or three pieces and put in a pan. Sprinkle with salt, barely cover with water and bring to the boil. Cook the potatoes covered for 20–25 minutes.

3 Drain the cooking water. Leave the potatoes in the open pan, shaking occasionally so that the steam escapes, or put a tea towel or kitchen paper between the lid and the pan to absorb the steam.

Tip: Boiled potatoes go well with most meat, fish or vegetable dishes with sauce.

Variation: For parsley potatoes, prepare the potatoes as above and toss in 20–30 g/¾–1 oz melted butter and 2 tablespoons of chopped parsley.

Potato pancakes

Preparation time:
about 45 minutes

1 kg/2¼ lb floury potatoes
1 onion
3 medium eggs
1 heaped teaspoon salt
40 g/1½ oz (6 tablespoons)
plain (all-purpose) flour
100 ml/3½ fl oz (½ cup) cooking
oil, e.g. sunflower oil

Per serving:
P: 11 g, F: 20 g, C: 37 g,
kJ: 1566, kcal: 373

1 Wash the potatoes, peel and rinse. Peel the onions. Grate the potatoes (photograph 1) and onion finely over a bowl. Add the eggs, salt and flour and mix well (photograph 2).

2 Heat a little oil in a pan. Spoon small quantities of the potato and onion mixture in the pan using a gravy ladle or tablespoon (photograph 3), press flat immediately and cook the potato pancakes on both sides over medium heat until the edge turns crispy brown.

3 Take the pancakes out of the pan, remove excess fat by dabbing them dry with kitchen paper and serve immediately, or keep in a warm place.

4 Make the rest of the pancakes in the same way.

Tip: Potato pancakes can be served with apple sauce or plum compote, herb or horseradish curd cheese or with smoked salmon with herb-flavoured crème fraîche and a green salad.
The potato pancakes will be even crisper if half the flour is replaced with 2–3 tablespoons rolled oats.

Variation 1: Put the fried pancakes on a baking sheet lined with greaseproof paper. Put 1–2 slices of tomatoes and 1 slice of mozzarella on top of each pancake, sprinkle some pepper on top and cook briefly in the preheated oven (top/bottom heat: about 220 °C/425 °F, fan oven: about 200 °C/400 °F, gas mark 7) until the cheese melts. Garnish with small basil leaves before serving.

Variation 2: To make potato pancakes with ham, cut 50 g/2 oz ham on the bone into thin strips and add to the potato and onion mixture together with 1–2 teaspoons marjoram. Alternatively, strips of ham may be added to crème fraîche and served with the potato pancakes.

Potato purée

Preparation time:
about 35 minutes

1 kg/2¼ lb floury potatoes
salt
50 g/2 oz (4 tablespoons) butter
or margarine
about 250 ml/8 fl oz (1 cup)
milk
grated nutmeg

Per serving:
P: 6 g, F: 13 g, C: 33 g,
kJ: 1160, kcal: 277

1 Wash the potatoes, peel, rinse, cut into pieces and put in a sauce-pan. Add some salt and just enough water to cover the potatoes, then bring to the boil. Cover and cook for about 15 minutes until done, drain and put them through a potato ricer or mash them with a potato masher. Add the butter or margarine.

2 Bring the milk to the boil and stir little by little into the potato mash, using a whisk or wooden spoon (the amount of milk will vary according to the type of potato).

3 Beat the mash with the whisk over low heat until it has a light, smooth consistency. Season with salt and nutmeg.

Note: Do not purée the potatoes with hand-held blender because they would become glutinous!

Tip: Potato purée can be served with celery escalopes (page 92), roast meat, meat balls, fish, or eggs in mustard sauce (page 140).

Variation 1: Use whipping cream instead of milk but omit the butter. Alternatively, leave out the butter, fry 100 g/3½ oz diced streaky bacon to release the fat and stir this into the potato purée.

Variation 2: Potato purée with garlic and herbs. Peel 1–2 cloves garlic and chop up. Melt the butter, add the garlic and sweat for about 5 minutes over low heat. Finally, stir the garlic butter into the potato purée together with 2 tablespoons chopped parsley and 1 tablespoon chopped chives.

Variation 3: Potato purée with cheese. Just before serving add 4 tablespoons grated, medium-aged Gouda or Emmental to the potato purée and sprinkle with 1 tablespoon chopped parsley or chervil.

Raw potato
dumplings (photograph)

Preparation time:
about 60 minutes;

12 dumplings

1.5 kg/3¼ lb firm cooking
potatoes
250 ml/8 fl oz (1 cup) milk
70 g/3 oz (4 tablespoons) butter
or margarine
salt
150 g/5 oz hard wheat semolina
flour
1 bread roll
salted water – 1 litre/1¾ pints
(4½ cups) water with 1 teaspoon
salt

Per serving:
P: 13 g, F: 18 g, C: 79 g,
kJ: 2242, kcal: 535

1 Wash the potatoes, peel, rinse and grate them into a bowl filled with cold water. Drain the grated potatoes in a sieve and press in a tea towel to squeeze out all the water.

2 Add 40 g/1½ oz (3 tablespoons) butter or margarine and 2 teaspoons salt to the milk and bring to the boil. Next stir in the semolina and briefly bring back to the boil. Then immediately add to the squeezed grated potatoes and form into a homogenous mass using a hand-held mixer with a kneading attachment. Check the seasoning and add salt if necessary.

3 Cut the roll into small cubes. Melt the remaining butter or margarine in a pan, add the diced roll and fry until brown, stirring occasionally.

4 Fill a saucepan with enough water for the dumplings to be able to "swim" in the liquid, add salt and bring to the boil. Make 12 dumplings from the grated potato mass, using your hands which you first moisten. Press a few fried bread croutons into each dumpling. Place the dumplings into the boiling salted water, bring back to the boil and cook covered for about 20 minutes with a lid (the water should bubble gently). Use a skimming ladle to remove the dumplings from the water when they are done. Drain them thoroughly.

Half-and-half
potato dumplings

Preparation time:
about 75 minutes,
excluding cooling time;

12 dumplings

1.25 g/2¾ lb firm cooking
potatoes
1 medium egg
65 g/2 oz (5 tablespoons) plain
(all-purpose) flour

1 Wash 750 g/1½ lb of the potatoes thoroughly and bring to the boil in a saucepan of water. Cover and cook for about 20–25 minutes. Drain the potatoes, rinse with cold water and peel. Then immediately push them through a potato ricer or mash with a potato masher. Leave to cool down, cover and refrigerate until the following day.

2 Wash the rest of the potatoes, peel, rinse and grate into a bowl of cold water. Put in a sieve to drain and press in a tea towel to squeeze out all the water. Add to the cooked potato. Add the egg, flour and salt, and knead until the mixture forms a smooth consistency.

continued on page 122 ⏩

1 teaspoon salt
salted water – 1 litre/1¾ pints
(4½ cups) water with 1 teaspoon
salt

Per serving:
P: 9 g, F: 2 g, C: 51 g,
kJ: 1116, kcal: 266

3 Shape 12 dumplings using your hands lightly coated with flour. Fill a large saucepan with enough water for the dumplings to be able to "swim" in the liquid. Add salt and bring to the boil. Put the dumplings in the boiling salted water, bring back to the boil and poach uncovered over low heat for about 20 minutes (the water should only move very slightly). When the dumplings are cooked, remove from the water with a skimming ladle and drain well.

Schupfnudeln (potato noodles)

Preparation time:
about 60 minutes,
excluding cooling time;

36 pieces

300 g/10 oz floury cooking
potatoes
salt
1 medium egg
100 g/3½ oz (1 cup) plain (all-purpose) flour
freshly ground pepper
grated nutmeg
salted water – 1 litre/1¾ pints
(4½ cups) water with 1 teaspoon
salt
30 g/1 oz (2 tablespoons) butter

Per serving:
P: 6 g, F: 8 g, C: 27 g,
kJ: 852, kcal: 203

1 Wash the potatoes, peel thinly, rinse and put in a saucepan. Add ½ teaspoon salt, add just enough water to cover the potatoes and bring to the boil. Cover and cook for about 20 minutes. Drain and dry the potatoes and put immediately through the potato ricer (photograph 1) or mash with a potato masher, then leave to cool down.

2 Stir the egg and flour into the potato purée and season with salt, pepper and nutmeg. Shape into finger-thick cylindrical rolls about 5 cm/2 in long, using your hands lightly coated with flour. Make the rolls slightly thinner at the ends (photograph 2).

3 Fill a large saucepan with enough water for the dumplings to be able to "swim" in the liquid and bring back to the boil. Put the dumplings in the boiling water, bring back to the boil and cook uncovered over low heat for 3–4 minutes (photograph 3). The water should only move very slightly.

4 Remove the dumplings from the water with a skimming ladle and leave to drain thoroughly. Melt the butter, add the dumplings and fry for 3–4 minutes, stirring occasionally.

Tip: Serve these dumplings with braised beef, goulash, Geschnetzeltes (thin slices of meat cooked in sauce, page 48) or sauerkraut (page 94).

Kastenpickert (yeast potato bread)

Preparation time: about
45 minutes, excluding rising,
baking and cooling time

Cooking time:
about 60 minutes;

8 servings

1 kg/2¼ lb floury potatoes
3 medium eggs
1 heaped teaspoon salt
125 ml/4 fl oz (½ cup) milk
500 g/18 oz (5 cups) plain (all-purpose) flour
1 packet dried yeast
250 g/9 oz raisins

In addition:
fat for the mould
200 ml/7 fl oz (⅞ cup) cooking oil, e.g. sunflower oil

Per serving:
P: 13 g, F: 29 g, C: 81 g,
kJ: 2685, kcal: 641

1 Wash the potatoes, peel thinly, rinse and grate finely (photograph 1). Leave to drain in a sieve, transfer to a mixing bowl, add the eggs and salt, and mix well.

2 Heat the milk in a small saucepan. Sieve the flour in a bowl, add the dried yeast and mix very well. Mix together the warm milk and flour and yeast mixture in two stages. Knead to make a smooth, homogenous consistency, using a hand-held mixer with kneading attachment.

3 Continue kneading the dough for about 5 minutes. Then cover and put in a warm place to rise (about 60 minutes).

4 Stir the raisins into the dough and put in a well-greased bread tin (35 x 11 cm/14 x 4½ in, photograph 2), cover and leave in a warm place to rise again for about 30 minutes. Preheat the oven at top and bottom and put the tin in the oven **for about 60 minutes**.

Top/bottom heat: about 180 °C/350 °F (preheated), Fan oven: about 160 °C/325 °F (not preheated), Gas mark 4 (not preheated).

5 Remove the pickert from the tin and leave to cool down on a wire tray. When cool cut into 24 slices.

6 Heat a little oil in a pan and fry the pickert slices on both sides until golden brown (photograph 3).

Tip: Serve the pickert with syrup, jam or apple sauce. It is also delicious with butter and it can be served with coffee.

Variation: Yeast pancakes (makes about 20). Make the dough as described above but use only 2 eggs. Finally, stir in the raisins. Fry in a pan, a few at a time. Spoon the dough mixture into the frying pan, press flat and fry the pancakes on both sides until golden brown. Drain briefly on kitchen paper. Serve the pancakes in the same way as pickert.

Spätzle

Preparation time:
about 35 minutes

250 g/9 oz (2½ cups) plain (all-purpose) flour
2 medium eggs
scant ½ teaspoon salt
about 3 tablespoons water
3 litres/5 pints (13 cups) water
3 teaspoons salt
40 g/1½ oz (3 tablespoons) butter

Per serving:
P: 10 g, F: 12 g, C: 45 g,
kJ: 1361, kcal: 325

1 Sieve the flour into a bowl. Add the eggs, salt and 5 tablespoons water. Knead all the ingredients together using a hand-held mixer with a kneading attachment (photograph 1) or wooden spoon, making sure that there are no lumps. Continue kneading until the dough begins to form air bubbles.

2 Bring 3 litres/5 pints (13 cups) water to the boil and add salt. Push the dough through a spätzle ricer or spätzle press (photograph 2) into the boiling water and poach for 3–5 minutes; the spätzle are done when they float to the surface.

3 Remove the spätzle from the water using a skimming ladle, transfer to a sieve or colander, rinse under cold water and drain. Brown the butter in a pan and toss the spätzle in it (photograph 3).

Tip: Serve spätzle as an accompaniment to braised beef, goulash or escalopes (page 50).

Variation 1: To make spätzle coated with breadcrumbs, melt 30 g/1 oz (2 tablespoons) butter in a pan, stir in 2 tablespoons breadcrumbs and pour over the spätzle.

Variation 2: To make spätzle with fried onions (photograph), peel 3 onions, cut into rings, brown in melted butter or margarine and pour over the spätzle just before serving.

Variation 3: To make cheese spätzle, make the spätzle as described above but using 400 g/14 oz wheat flour, 4 medium eggs, 1 level teaspoon salt and 150 ml/5 fl oz (⅝ cup) water. Arrange the drained spätzle and 200 g/7 oz grated Emmental cheese in layers in a greased gratin dish (the top layer should be cheese). Put the dish in the preheated oven (top and bottom heat) at a temperature of about 200 °C/400 °F, fan oven about 180 °C/350 °F, gas mark 6 and bake the cheese spätzle for about 20 minutes. Sprinkle the cheese spätzle with fried onion rings (made from 4 onions) and serve with a mixed salad as a main dish.

Maultaschen (stuffed Swabian pockets)

Preparation time:
about 75 minutes, without
baking and cooling time;

24 pieces

Preparation for the spinach
filling:
600 g/1¼ lb frozen leaf spinach

For the dough:
300 g/12 oz (3 cups) plain (all-
purpose) flour
2 medium eggs
3 tablespoons water
some salt

For the spinach filling:
2 onions
2 cloves garlic
4 teaspoons cooking oil,
e.g. sunflower or olive oil
salt
freshly ground pepper
grated nutmeg
1 yolk of 1 medium egg

1 white of 1 medium egg
1.5 litres/2¾ pints (7 cups)
vegetable or meat stock

Per serving:
P: 18 g, F: 11 g, C: 57 g,
kJ: 1686, kcal: 402

1 Defrost the spinach following the instructions on the packet to make the spinach stuffing.

2 To make the dough, sieve the flour into a bowl, then add the eggs, water and salt. Knead all the ingredients together to make a smooth dough, using a hand-held mixer with kneading attachment. Cover and leave to rest for about 40 minutes.

3 Meanwhile, squeeze the defrosted spinach to remove all the water and coarsely chop. Peel and chop the onions and garlic.

4 Heat the oil in a pan, add the chopped onions and garlic and fry while stirring. Then add the spinach, stir, cover and braise over low heat for about 3 minutes. Season with salt, pepper and nutmeg and leave to cool a little. Finally stir in the egg yolk.

5 Roll out the dough thinly on a floured work surface and cut out squares 10 x 10 cm/4 x 4 in from the dough. Put a little stuffing on each square. Beat the egg white with a fork and brush along the edges of each square. Fold the squares into triangles and press the edges together.

6 Heat the vegetable or meat stock in a pan. Put half the stuffed pockets in the liquid and poach uncovered over medium heat for about 15 minutes. Remove the stuffed pockets from the water with a skimming ladle and keep in a warm place. Repeat the same operation with the rest of the stuffed pockets.

7 Serve the stuffed pockets with a little stock in soup bowls.

Tip: Drain the cooked stuffed pockets and fry on both sides in melted butter. Then serve with breadcrumbs browned in butter and onion rings (from 6–8 onions) fried in clarified butter or vegetable oil (photograph).

Variation: Pockets stuffed with minced meat. Peel and chop 1 onion. Heat 1 tablespoon vegetable oil in a pan. Add the chopped onion and fry over medium heat. Add the fried onion to 300 g/10 oz minced meat (half beef, half pork), 1 medium egg, yolk of 1 medium egg and 2 table-spoons chopped parsley, mix well and season with salt and pepper. Stuff the dough squares and poach as described above.

Breadcrumb dumplings

Preparation time:
about 50 minutes,
excluding cooling time;

12 dumplings

50 g/2 oz streaky bacon
2 onions
2 teaspoons cooking oil,
e.g. sunflower oil
300 g/10 oz (about 8 pieces)
dry rolls
300 ml/10 fl oz (1¼ cups) milk
30 g/1 oz (2 tablespoons) butter
4 medium eggs
4 teaspoons chopped parsley
salt
salted water – 1 litre/1¾ pints
(4½ cups) water with 1 teaspoon
salt

Per serving:
P: 19 g, F: 20 g, C: 51 g,
kJ: 1922, kcal: 459

1 Cut the bacon into cubes. Peel the onions and chop finely. Heat the oil in a pan, add the diced bacon and fry until crisp. Add the chopped onions and continue frying over low heat while stirring.

2 Cut the rolls into small cubes and put in a bowl. Heat the milk with the butter, pour over the diced rolls (photograph 1) and stir well. Now stir in the onion and bacon mixture together with the fat from the frying (photograph 2) and leave to cool.

3 Beat the eggs with the parsley, stir into the cooled onion and bacon mixture and season with salt. Make 12 dumplings from this mixture, using your hands, lightly floured (photograph 3). Fill a large saucepan with enough boiling salted water for the dumplings to be able to "swim" in the liquid. Put the dumplings in the boiling water, bring back to the boil and poach uncovered for about 20 minutes (the water should only move very slightly). When the dumplings are done, remove from the water with a skimming ladle and drain well.

Tip: Serve with roasts.
Leave the rolls to dry for 2–3 days before using them to make the dumplings.

Variation: Pretzel dumplings. Use pretzels instead of rolls and add 1 tablespoon of chopped chives to the dumpling mixture.

Potato bake

Preparation time:
about 75 minutes,
excluding cooling time

Cooking time:
about 35 minutes

1 kg/2¼ lb firm cooking
potatoes
5 hard-boiled eggs
3 smoked sausages,
100 g/3½ oz each
salt
freshly ground pepper
300 g/10 oz sour cream
30 g/1 oz breadcrumbs
50 g/2 oz (4 tablespoons) butter

Per serving:
P: 29 g, F: 53 g, C: 42 g,
kJ: 3192, kcal: 762

1 Wash the potatoes thoroughly, put in a pan filled with water and bring to the boil. Cover and cook for about 20–25 minutes. Drain the potatoes, then place them in cold water and drain. Peel immediately and leave to cool down. Meanwhile, preheat the oven.

2 Shell the eggs and slice them. Then slice the potatoes and the smoked sausages. Arrange these ingredients in alternate layers in a shallow gratin dish. Sprinkle salt and pepper on layers of sliced potatoes and sliced eggs. Finish with a layer of potatoes.

3 Season the soured cream with salt and pepper, mix well and pour over the potatoes. Sprinkle the breadcrumbs on top and dot with knobs of butter. Bake the potato gratin uncovered in the oven **for about 35 minutes**.

Top/bottom heat: about 200 °C/400 °F (preheated), Fan oven: about 180 °C/350 °F (not preheated), Gas mark 6 (preheated).

Tip: Serve potato bake with a carrot and apple salad (page 106). If you use thick soured cream you can make it less thick by adding 5 tablespoons milk.

Variation: Potato and courgette bake with cabanossi (photograph). Instead of hard-boiled eggs use 300 g/10 oz courgettes. Wash the courgettes, wipe dry, cut both ends and slice. Sprinkle with salt and leave for about 10 minutes. Use 300 g/10 oz cabanossi (garlic sausage) instead of the smoked sausages and cut into slices. Pat the courgettes dry and arrange with the sliced potatoes and cabanossi so that they overlap. Sprinkle pepper on the potato and courgette slices. Beat together the sour cream and 2 medium eggs, season with salt and pepper and pour over the gratin. Sprinkle breadcrumbs on top, dot with knobs of butter and bake as above.

Pancake gratin

Preparation time: about
100 minutes, excluding batter
resting and cooling time

Cooking time:
about 35 minutes

For the pancakes:
185 g/6½ oz (1½ cups) plain
(all-purpose) flour
3 medium eggs
1 pinch sugar
1 pinch salt
225 ml/7½ fl oz (1 cup) milk
150 ml/5 fl oz (⅝ cup) mineral
water
40 g/1½ oz margarine
or 3 tablespoons cooking oil,
e.g. sunflower oil

For the filling:
2 onions
2 cloves garlic
250 g/9 oz carrots
30 g/1 oz (2 tablespoons)
margarine or 2 tablespoons
cooking oil, e.g. sunflower oil
450 g/1 lb frozen leaf spinach
salt, pepper
grated nutmeg

For the sauce:
200 g/7 oz fromage frais
1 medium egg
salt, pepper

In addition:
fat for the mould
125 g/4½ oz mozzarella cheese
some small-leaved basil

Per serving:
P: 29 g, F: 52 g, C: 43 g,
kJ: 3151, kcal: 752

1 Sieve the flour for the pancakes into a mixing bowl and make a well in the centre. Whisk together the eggs, sugar, salt, milk and mineral water and pour a little of this mixture into the well. Starting from the middle, mix together a little of the egg mixture and the flour, adding the rest of the egg mixture little by little, making sure that there are no lumps. Leave the batter to stand for 20–30 minutes.

2 Heat some of the margarine or oil in a pan and pour a thin layer of batter into the pan. As soon as the edges turn golden yellow, carefully turn over the pancake using a wooden spatula. Alternatively, slide the pancake onto a plate and return to the pan on the other side. Fry the second side until it is golden yellow, too. Add a little more oil or margarine before turning the pancake. Make sure the pancake is golden brown on both sides. Make 6–8 pancakes (depending on the size of the frying pan), stacking the pancakes on top of each other and let them cool down.

3 To make the stuffing, peel and chop the onions and garlic. Peel the carrots and cut off the green leaves and tips, then wash, drain and cut into small dice.

4 Heat the oil or margarine in a pan. Add the chopped onions and garlic and fry while stirring. Add the carrots and frozen spinach, cover and cook over low heat for about 10–15 minutes until the spinach is defrosted, stirring occasionally. Preheat the oven. Boil way any excess liquid in the vegetable mixture. Season with salt, pepper and nutmeg and leave to cool.

5 Meanwhile mix together the fromage frais, milk and egg and season with salt and pepper.

6 Put the pancakes next to each other on the worktop and spoon the stuffing onto each pancake. Roll them up and arrange next to each other in a shallow, greased gratin dish (about 30 x 24 cm/12 x 10 in). Pour the sauce over each one. Cut the mozzarella into thin strips and scatter on top. Bake uncovered in the oven **for about 35 minutes**.

Top/bottom heat: about 200 °C/400 °F (preheated), Fan oven: about 180 °C/350 °F (preheated), Gas mark 6 (preheated).

7 Garnish with basil leaves just before serving.

continued on page 136 ⫸

Variation: Pancake gratin with sheep's cheese and raisins. Add 50 g/ 2 oz raisins and fry with the vegetables. Season the vegetables with salt, pepper, ground cumin and ground coriander seeds. Prepare the sauce with puréed sheep's or goat's cheese instead of fromage frais. Make the gratin as described in the recipe and bake.

Rice and vegetable gratin

Preparation time:
about 50 minutes

Cooking time:
about 25 minutes

300 g/10 oz carrots
4 teaspoons cooking oil,
e.g. sunflower oil
250 g/9 oz long-grain rice
4 teaspoons curry powder
500 ml/17 fl oz (2¼ cups)
vegetable stock
40 g/1½ oz butter or margarine
300 g/10 oz frozen peas
salt
freshly ground pepper
1 pinch sugar
2 medium eggs
200 ml/7 fl oz (⅞ cup) whipping
cream
grated nutmeg
125 g/4½ oz grated, medium
mature Gouda cheese

Per serving:
P: 23 g, F: 41 g, C: 64 g,
kJ: 3042, kcal: 726

1 Peel the carrots and cut off the green leaves and tips. Wash the carrots, drain and cut into small dice.

2 Heat the oil in a pan. Add the rice and fry until transparent. Sprinkle the curry powder over the rice and fry briefly. Add the vegetable stock, bring to the boil, cover and cook over low heat for about 10 minutes. Preheat the oven.

3 Meanwhile melt the butter or margarine. Add the diced carrots and fry. Stir in the peas and season with salt, pepper and sugar. Mix the rice and vegetables together and put in a shallow gratin dish.

4 Whisk the eggs into the cream, season with salt, pepper and nutmeg and stir in the cheese. Pour the egg and cream mixture over the rice and vegetables in the gratin dish. Bake in the oven without a lid **for about 25 minutes**.

Top/bottom heat: about 180 °C/350 °F (preheated), Fan oven: about 160 °C/325 °F (preheated), Gas mark 4 (not preheated).

Tip: Serve the rice and vegetable gratin with green salad, cold roast or ham.
You can use a similar amount of brown rice, but in this case the cooking time for the rice will be about 20 minutes.

Variation: Rice and vegetable gratin with chicken fillets (photograph). Rinse 300 g/10 oz chicken fillets under cold running water, pat dry, cut into strips and brown on all sides in the oil. Season with salt and pepper and remove from the pan. Fry the rice in the remaining cooking fat until transparent and continue as indicated above. Stir the chicken into the rice and vegetable mixture, put in a gratin dish and bake as indicated above.

Stuffed eggs

Preparation time:
about 25 minutes

4 hard-boiled medium eggs
1 tablespoon mayonnaise
1 slightly heaped teaspoon mustard
salt
freshly ground pepper
1 pinch sugar
some salad leaves
8 preserved anchovy fillets
about 3 pickled gherkins
some cocktail tomatoes
chopped parsley

Per serving:
P: 9 g, F: 9 g, C: 2 g,
kJ: 523, kcal: 125

1 Shell the eggs, cut in half lengthways and remove the yolks (photograph 1). Rub the egg yolks through a sieve (photograph 2), add the mayonnaise and mustard and stir into a smooth mass (photograph 3). Season with salt, pepper and sugar. Put the mixture in a piping bag with a large star-shaped nozzle and squeeze into the hollows of the egg halves.

2 Wash the lettuce leaves and spin dry. Pat the sardine fillets dry. Drain the gherkins and cut into strips. Wash the cherry tomatoes, wipe dry and cut in half. Arrange the egg halves on the lettuce leaves. Garnish with the anchovy fillets, strips of gherkin and cherry tomatoes. Sprinkle with parsley before serving.

Variation 1: Eggs stuffed with curried curd cheese. Take 50 g/2 oz fromage frais, 1 teaspoon crème fraîche and ½ teaspoon curry powder and stir into the egg yolks rubbed through a sieve. Season with salt, pepper and sugar and fill the egg halves with this mixture. Garnish with 1–2 tablespoons crab or shrimps, some dill and slices of lemon.

Variation 2: Eggs with Parmesan stuffing. Stir 1 tablespoon crème fraîche, 1 tablespoon finely grated Parmesan and a few chopped pink pepper berries into the egg yolks rubbed through a sieve. Season with salt and pepper and fill the egg halves with the mixture. Garnish with 1 tablespoon roasted pine nuts and 1 tablespoon chopped rocket.

Variation 3: Eggs with herb curd cheese stuffing. Stir 1 tablespoon each crème fraîche and herb curd cheese into the egg yolk rubbed through a sieve. Season with salt and sugar. Spoon into the egg halves and garnish with about 100 g/3½ oz coloured peppers, cut into strips.

Variation 4: Eggs with tomato flavoured curd cheese. Mix together 2 tablespoons curd cheese, 1–2 teaspoons tomato purée and 1 teaspoon drained, finely chopped capers and stir into the egg yolk rubbed through a sieve. Season with salt and sugar, fill the egg halves with this mixture and garnish with 50 g/2 oz ham cut into thin strips.

Boiled eggs

Preparation time:
about 10 minutes

4 fresh medium eggs

Per serving:
P: 7 g, F: 6 g, C: 0 g,
kJ: 355, kcal: 85

1 Pierce the eggs at the blunt end with a needle or egg-pricker so that they do not crack when they boil. Bring some water to the boil in a small saucepan.

2 Place the eggs on a spoon or skimming ladle and lower them carefully into the boiling water (the eggs should be covered by the water). Bring the water to the boil again and boil the eggs uncovered over low heat. For soft-boiled medium eggs, the cooking time is 5 minutes. For medium-boiled eggs, the cooking time is 8 minutes. For hard-boiled eggs, the cooking time is 10 minutes. Add 1 minute to the cooking time if the eggs are large.

3 Remove the eggs from the water with a spoon or skimming ladle and dip in cold water so that they easier to shell.

Tip: If the eggs have come straight from the refrigerator, add 1 more minute to the cooking time. Very cold eggs should be pre-warmed in lukewarm water to prevent the shells from cracking.

Eggs with mustard sauce (photograph)

Preparation time:
about 20 minutes

25 g/1 oz (2 tablespoons) butter or margarine
20 g/¾ oz (3 tablespoons) plain (all-purpose) flour
each 125 ml/4 fl oz (½ cup) vegetable stock, milk and whipping cream
2 tablespoons medium-hot mustard
salt
freshly ground pepper
some lemon juice

8 hard-boiled medium eggs

Per serving:
P: 17 g, F: 29 g, C: 7 g,
kJ: 1509, kcal: 360

1 Melt the butter or margarine in a pan. Add the flour and stir over heat until the mixture turns a pale yellow. Add the stock and stir vigourously using a whisk, making sure that there are no lumps. Add also the milk and the whipping cream while stirring.

2 Bring the sauce to the boil and simmer gently for about 5 minutes without the lid on, stirring occasionaly. Finally, stir in the mustard and season the sauce with salt, pepper and lemon juice.

3 Shell the eggs, cut in half lenghtways and put into the sauce.

Pancakes

Preparation time:
about 40 minutes,
excluding resting time;

about 7 pancakes

250 g/9 oz plain (all-purpose)
flour
4 medium eggs
2 teaspoons sugar
1 pinch salt
375 ml/12 fl oz (1½ cups) milk
125 ml/4 fl oz (½ cup) mineral
water
5 tablespoons cooking oil,
e.g. sunflower oil or 80 g/3 oz
(6 tablespoons) clarified butter

Per serving:
P: 10 g, F: 17 g, C: 29 g,
kJ: 1290, kcal: 308

1 Sieve the flour in a bowl and make a well in the centre. Beat together the eggs, milk and mineral water using a whisk and stir in the sugar and salt. Pour a little of this mixture in the well and mix with the flour around. Now add the rest of the egg-mixture little by little to the flour, making sure that there are no lumps. Let the batter rest for 20–30 minutes.

2 Heat the oil or clarified butter in a non-stick frying pan (diameter about 24 cm/9½ in) and pour a thin layer of batter to coat the base of the pan. As soon as the edges turn golden yellow, turn the pancakes very gently with a wide spatula or slide the pancake onto plate and return to the pan on the other side. Cook until the second side is golden yellow. Add a little more fat before cooking the second side.

3 Continue making the rest of the pancakes in the same way, stirring the batter each time before making each pancake.

Tip: You can serve pancakes with stewed fruit, cinnamon sugar, maple syrup or fruit. The pancakes will be more delicate and lighter if you separate the eggs and only use the yolks in the batter. Shortly before making the pancakes beat the egg whites stiff and fold into the batter.
Keep the pancakes you have already made in a warm oven, heated top and bottom to 80 °C/180 °F or 60 °C/14 °F if it is a fan oven. Sprinkle each pancake with a little sugar before stacking them. This will prevent them from sticking together.

Variation 1: Apple pancakes (photograph). Make the batter as described above. Wash 1 kg/2¼ lb of slightly sharp apples (for instance Bramleys), peel, cut into quarters, remove the cores and cut lengthways into thin slices. Divide into 7 portions. Heat a small amount of the oil or clarified butter in the pan, add 1 portion of the sliced apples and fry for 2–3 minutes. Then pour a thin layer of batter on top and cook over medium heat, now and again lifting the pancake from the bottom of the pan to cook as described above. Make the rest of the pancakes as indicated above. Serve the pancakes with cinnamon sugar.

Variation 2: Bacon pancakes. Make the batter as described above, but only with 1 pinch of sugar. Cut 200 g/7 oz bacon into slices, and for each pancake fry a portion in the hot oil or clarified butter until golden brown. Pour the batter on top and cook as indicated above. Proceed with the rest of the batter and bacon in the same way. Serve the bacon pancakes with a green salad.

Pork fillet toast
with cheese (photograph top)

Preparation time:
about 30 minutes

300 g / 10 oz pork fillet
4 teaspoons cooking oil,
e.g. sunflower oil
salt
freshly ground pepper
4 slices bacon, 60 g/2 oz each
4 slices white bread
30 g/1 oz (2 tablespoons) butter
200 g/7 oz Camembert
some salad leaves, e.g. lettuce,
endive salad
coarsely ground pepper
(optional)

In addition:
baking parchment

Per serving:
P: 32 g, F: 22 g, C: 10 g,
kJ: 1536, kcal: 367

1 Preheat the oven. Rinse the pork fillet under cold running water, pat dry and cut into 8 slices. Heat the oil in a pan. Add the pork slices and fry on each side for about 2 minutes, season with salt and pepper, remove from the pan and keep in a warm place.

2 Fry the bacon briefly in the remaining fat and remove from the pan. Toast the slices of bread and spread with butter. Cut the Camembert into slices.

3 Rinse the lettuce leaves, pat dry and arrange on the toasted bread. Then garnish with the slices of bacon, pork fillet and camembert.

4 Put the pieces of toast on a baking sheet lined with greaseproof paper. Put the baking sheet with the toast under the oven grill until the cheese begins to melt. Sprinkle with pepper if desired.

Variation 1: Cheese on toast with spring onions (photograph bottom right). Wash 2 tomatoes, pat dry, remove the stalks and cut the tomatoes into slices. Cut off the root ends and dark green leaves of the spring onions, wash and drain. Then cut to the length of the 4 slices of bread and cut in half. Toast the slices of bread, spread with 60 g/2 oz peanut butter. Then arrange 1 slice of roast meat (20 g/¾ oz each), 2–3 slices of tomatoes, ½ spring onion and 1 slice of Danish butter cheese (30 g/1 oz each) on top. Put the garnished toast on a baking sheet lined with baking parchment and place under the preheated oven grill until the cheese begins to melt.

Variation 2: Hawaiian toast (photograph bottom left). Toast 4 slices of bread and spread with 30 g/1 oz (2 tablespoons) butter. Garnish each piece of toast with 1 slice cooked ham (40 g/1½ oz each), 1 slice pineapple from a can (80 g/3 oz each) and 1 slice of cheese, for instance young Gouda (60 g/2 oz each). Put the garnished pieces of toast on a baking sheet lined with baking parchment and put in the oven preheated top and bottom to about 200 °C/400 °F, fan oven about 180 °C/ 350 °F, Gas mark 6, for about 8 minutes.

Tip: Serve with a mixed green salad (page 104) or iceberg salad. If you do not have an oven grill, put the pieces of toast in a preheated oven until the cheese begins to melt (see variations for the temperatures).

Bavarian pudding (photograph bottom)

Preparation time:
about 40 minutes,
excluding cooling time;

4–5 servings

1 vanilla pod
250 ml/8 fl oz (1 cup) milk
6 leaves white gelatine
yolks of 3 medium eggs
75 g/3 oz sugar
250 ml/8 fl oz (1 cup) chilled
whipping cream

Per serving:
P: 8 g, F: 24 g, C: 21 g,
kJ: 1383, kcal: 330

1 Cut open the vanilla pod. Scoop out the flesh with the back of a knife, put in the pan together with the milk and bring to the boil. Soak the gelatine in cold water, following the instructions on the packet.

2 Beat together the egg yolk and sugar in a stainless steel bowl or saucepan using a whisk. Now stir the hot milk into the egg and sugar mixture. Put the bowl or saucepan in a bain-marie and heat while whisking continuously until the mixture thickens and turns white (neither the water nor mixture should be allowed to boil or the mixture may curdle). Remove the mixture from the bain-marie.

3 Squeeze the gelatine to remove as much water as possible and dissolve in the mixture while it is still hot. Then strain the mixture through a fine sieve and allow to cool, stirring occasionally. As soon as the mixture begins to set, whip the cream until stiff and fold into the setting mixture. Take 4–5 ramekins or cups, each with a capacity of 150–200 ml/5–7 fl oz ($\frac{5}{8}$–$\frac{7}{8}$ cup). Rinse them in cold water, fill with the mixture and refrigerate for about 3 hours until set.

4 Carefully loosen the pudding along the edges with the point of a knife. Place the ramekins or cups briefly in hot water and turn the puddings out onto the plates. Garnish to taste.

Tip: Serve Bavarian pudding with whipped cream and fruit, fruit purée or chocolate sauce.

Variation 1: Bavarian cappuccino cream pudding (photograph top). Dissolve 5 teaspoons instant espresso powder with the gelatine in the egg yolk and milk mixture and continue as described above. Fill cappuccino cups with this mixture and refrigerate. Before serving, beat 125 ml/4 fl oz ($\frac{1}{2}$ cup) whipping cream, put on top of the pudding to imitate the froth of a cappuccino and sprinkle with cocoa powder.

Variation 2: Bavarian orange cream. Add 3 teaspoons orange liqueur to the strained egg yolk and milk mixture and proceed as indicated above. Put the mixture in glass bowls or glasses, garnish with strips of orange peel (from 2–3 oranges) and refrigerate.

Variation 3: Bavarian chocolate cream. Chop up 150 g/5 oz plain chocolate, add to the egg yolk and milk mixture before adding the gelatine and dissolve into the mixture while stirring. Then dissolve the gelatine (use only 4 leaves because the pudding would set too firmly otherwise) and proceed as described above. The quantities make 6 servings of 150 ml/5 fl oz ($\frac{5}{8}$ cup) each.

Semolina pudding

Preparation time:
about 15 minutes,
excluding cooling time

½ vanilla pod
500 ml / 17 fl oz (2¼ cups) milk
75 g / 3 oz sugar
grated peel of ½ untreated
lemon
50 g / 2 oz soft wheat semolina
flour
1 medium egg

Per serving:
P: 7 g, F: 6 g, C: 34 g,
kJ: 925, kcal: 221

1 Cut open the vanilla pod lengthways (photograph 1) and scoop out the flesh with the back of a knife. Add the sugar, lemon peel, vanilla pod and flesh to the milk in a pan and bring to the boil. Add the semolina to the milk, stirring continuously (photograph 2). Bring to the boil and cook for about 1 minute while stirring.

2 Take the pan from the heat and remove the vanilla pod. Separate the egg and stir the egg yolk into the milk and semolina mixture. Beat the egg white stiff and fold carefully into the hot pudding.

3 Rinse the mould, bowl or ramekins in cold water and fill with the semolina pudding. Leave to cool and then refrigerate for about 3 hours.

4 Carefully loosen the pudding around the edges and turn out onto a plate (photograph 3).

Note: Only use very fresh eggs; check the sell-by date! Keep the pudding refrigerated and eat within 24 hours.

Tip: Serve semolina pudding with fresh fruit and whipping cream, stewed plums or puréed apricots.
Because the semolina mixture can spatter while cooking, it is advisable to use a spoon or whisk with a long handle for stirring.

Variation 1: Polenta pudding. Add sugar, lemon zest, vanilla pod and flesh to the milk together with 20 g/¾ oz (1½ tablespoons) butter and bring to the boil. Use polenta flour instead of semolina and proceed as described above.

Variation 2: Semolina curd cheese pudding. After you have added the stiffly beaten egg white, fold in 125 g/4½ oz curd cheese into the luke-warm pudding; add more sugar if desired.

Variation 3: Semolina pudding with cinnamon. Use 1 cinnamon stick instead of the vanilla pod.

Frothy wine sauce

Preparation time:
about 10 minutes;

4–6 servings

1 medium egg
yolk from 1 medium egg
60 g/2 oz sugar
125 ml/4 fl oz (½ cup) dry white
wine

Per serving:
P: 3 g, F: 3 g, C: 15 g,
kJ: 507, kcal: 121

1 Whisk together the egg and egg yolk and white wine in a stainless steel bowl or stainless steel saucepan.

2 Put the bowl with this mixture in a hot bain-marie over medium heat. Whisk with a hand-held mixer with whisk attachment, set at the lowest setting, until the mixture becomes thick and frothy. The mixture should almost double in volume. Do not let the water or the mixture boil because this may make the sauce curdle. Serve the sauce immediately.

Note: Use only very fresh eggs which are not more than 5 days old; check the sell-by date! Store the sauce in the refrigerator and eat within 24 hours.

Tip: Delicious with fruit salad (page 156) or ice cream.

Variation 1: Alcohol-free frothy sauce. Use 125 ml/4 fl oz (½ cup) apple juice and 2 tablespoons lemon juice instead of wine.

Variation 2: Zabaglione. Take yolks of 3 medium eggs, 60 g/2 oz sugar and 125 ml/4 fl oz (½ cup) Marsala (Italian dessert wine) and make the sauce as indicated above.

Swiss rice (photograph)

Preparation time:
about 40 minutes,
excluding cooling time

For the rice cream:
500 ml/17 fl oz (2¼ cups) milk
1 pinch salt
50 g/2 oz sugar
2–3 drops vanilla essence
in 1 tablespoon sugar
pudding rice (round grain rice)
200 ml/7 fl oz (⅞ cup) chilled
whipping cream

For the strawberry sauce:
500 g/18 oz strawberries
2–3 drops vanilla essence
in 1 tablespoon sugar
25 g/1 oz sugar

Per serving:
P: 6 g, F: 17 g, C: 46 g,
kJ: 1528, kcal: 365

1 To make the creamed rice, add the salt, sugar and vanilla sugar to the milk in a saucepan and bring to the boil. Add the rice and bring to the boil again while stirring. Cover and cook over low heat for 20 minutes, stirring occasionally; the rice should still have a kernel firm to the bite. Leave to cool down a little, cover and refrigerate.

2 Whip the cream and fold into the cold rice. Put the creamed rice in a bowl and refrigerate until served.

3 To make the strawberry sauce, wash the strawberries, drain and remove the stalks. Purée 400 g/14 oz of the strawberries and stir in the vanilla sugar and sugar. Slice the rest of the strawberries. Serve the creamed rice with the strawberry sauce and sliced strawberries.

Tip: This dish will feed 3 as a sweet meal.

Curd cheese with fruit (photograph)

Preparation time:
about 20 minutes,
excluding cooling time

1 can of peach halves, drained
weight 450 g/1 lb
grated zest of ½ untreated lime
or lemon
4 teaspoons lime or lemon juice
500 g/18 oz curd cheese
150 g/5 oz natural yogurt,
3.5% fat
2–3 tablespoons sugar
2–3 drops vanilla essence
in 1 tablespoon sugar

Per serving:
P: 18 g, F: 5 g, C: 38 g,
kJ: 1162, kcal: 277

1 Drain the peach halves in a colander, cut into small dice and mix together with the lime or lemon zest and juice.

2 Now whisk together curd cheese, yoghurt, sugar and vanilla sugar. Pour half of this mixture into a bowl. Arrange the diced peach halves on top, then cover with the rest of the curd cheese mixture. Refrigerate for at least 30 minutes before serving.

Tip: Garnish with lemon balm leaves before serving. This is a very reasonably-priced dessert for parties. 50 g/2 oz roast grated coconut may also be added: sprinkle half over the peach mixture and the rest on top of the curd cheese.

Variation: Chocolate curd cheese with bananas (photograph). Break 100 g/3½ oz plain chocolate into small pieces and melt in a bowl placed in a bain-marie over low heat. Add 4–6 tablespoons milk or whipping cream to 500 g/18 oz low fat curd cheese and stir until the mixture is smooth and homogenous. Stir in 2–3 drops natural vanilla essence in 1 tablespoon sugar, the melted chocolate and 1½ tablespoons sugar. Peel 4 small ripe bananas and put 1 banana on each plate. Put the curd cheese in a pastry bag with a large star-shaped nozzle and squeeze in whorls along the banana. If desired, garnish with praliné, roasted, peeled and flaked almonds or chocolate crumbs before serving.

Baked apples

Preparation time:
about 60 minutes,
excluding soaking time

Cooking time:
about 40 minutes;

8 servings

2 teaspoons raisins
about 100 ml/3½ fl oz (½ cup)
rum
8 apples, e.g. Cox
20 g/¾ oz soft butter
20 g/¾ oz sugar
2–3 drops vanilla essence
in 1 tablespoon sugar

1 Soak the raisins overnight in 2 tablespoons of rum.

2 Preheat the oven at the top and bottom. Wash the apples, wipe dry, remove the stalks and cores without pushing through. Arrange the apples in a well-greased gratin dish or on small heat-resistant plates.

3 Using a spoon, mix together the butter, vanilla sugar, ground almonds and soaked raisins. Fill the cored apples with this mixture using a teaspoon. Sprinkle the flaked almonds on top and press in slightly. Pour the rest of the rum over the apples. Put the dish or individual plates on a shelf in the oven for about 40 minutes.

Top/bottom heat: about 200 °C/400 °F (preheated), Fan oven: about 180° C/350 °F (not preheated), Gas mark 6 (not preheated).

continued on page 154 ⫸

4 teaspoons peeled ground almonds

4 teaspoons peeled coarsely dropped almonds

icing sugar

In addition:
fat for the form

Per serving:
P: 1 g, F: 4 g, C: 20 g,
kJ: 644, kcal: 154

4 Serve the baked apples hot and sprinkle with icing sugar just before serving.

Tip: Serve the baked apples with vanilla sauce (page 160) or lightly whipping cream. Ideal for pudding or at tea time.

Variation: Baked apples without alcohol. Soak the raisins in orange or apple juice, drain and proceed as indicated above. Instead of pouring rum over the apples, use orange or apple juice.

Red fruit pudding

Preparation time:
about 20 minutes,
excluding cooling time;

6 servings

250 g/9 oz blackberries
250 g/9 oz red currants
250 g/9 oz raspberries
250 g/9 oz strawberries
(all fruits weighed after being prepared)
35 g/1¼ oz cornflour (cornstarch)
100 g/3½ oz sugar
500 ml/17 fl oz (2¼ cups) fruit juice, e.g. sour cherry or red currant juice

Per serving:
P: 3 g, F: 1 g, C: 40 g,
kJ: 813, kcal: 194

1 Sort out the blackberries, wash carefully and drain thoroughly. Wash the red currants, drain well and remove from the stalks. Sort out the raspberries but do not wash. Wash the strawberries, drain, remove the stalks and cut into halves or quarters depending on the size.

2 Mix the cornflour with the sugar, add 4 tablespoons of the juice and stir well. Bring the rest of the juice to the boil in a saucepan. Stir in the juice and cornflour mixture, bring to the boil and remove the saucepan from the heat. Add the fruit and stir well. Put the red fruit pudding in a glass bowl or in pudding bowls and refrigerate.

Tip: Serve red fruit pudding with vanilla sauce (page 160) or cream. When served as a pudding or as a sweet meal with milk (in which case it will feed 4 people). It is an ideal party dessert.
You can also make this red fruit pudding with deep-frozen fruit. In this case, stir the deep-frozen fruit in the hot, thickened sauce.

Variation: Green fruit pudding. Wash 500 g/18 oz gooseberries, drain thoroughly and remove the stalks and any leaves. Peel 250 g/9 oz kiwi fruits, halve and cut into small pieces. Wash 250 g/9 oz seedless white grapes, drain well, remove the stalks and cut the larger grapes in half. Mix 20 g/¾ oz cornflour with 150 g/5 oz sugar. From 375 ml/12 fl oz (1½ cups) white grape juice, take 4 tablespoons and add to the cornflour and sugar mixture, then stir well. Bring the rest of the juice to the boil, stir in the cornflour and juice mixture and bring to the boil. Stir in the gooseberries and grapes, bring briefly to the boil, remove the pan from the heat and stir in the kiwi fruit. Put in a bowl and refrigerate.

Fruit salad

Preparation time:
about 30 minutes;

6 servings

1 apple
1 small mango
1 nectarine
1 peach
1 orange
1 kiwi fruit
1 banana
100 g/3½ oz strawberries
2 tablespoons lemon juice
2 teaspoons sugar or honey
(to taste)
30 g/1 oz chopped walnuts,
hazelnut kernels or almonds

Per serving:
P: 2 g, F: 3 g, C: 22 g,
kJ: 548, kcal: 131

1 Wash the apple, peel, cut into quarters and remove the core. Peel the mango, cut in half and remove the stone. Wash the nectarine and peach, wipe dry, cut in half and remove the stones. Cut all the fruit into pieces. Peel the orange so that the white pith is also removed using a sharp knife and "fillet" the segments, removing the membrane surrounding each segment.

2 Peel the kiwi fruit and bananas and slice. Wash the strawberries, drain, remove the stalks and cut into pieces.

3 Stir the lemon juice into the fruit and add sugar to taste. Put the fruit salad intoa glass bowl and sprinkle with chopped walnuts, hazelnuts and almonds.

Tip: As a dessert, serve the fruit salad with cream, vanilla sauce (page 160) or ice cream. As a sweet meal, serve with hot semolina pudding (page 148) or rice pudding. The flavour of the fruit salad can be enhanced by adding a little orange liqueur. You can also stir 50 g/2 oz raisins or 1 tablespoon chopped peppermint leaves into the salad.

Variation: Fruit salad can be varied endlessly according to the season and taste. In winter some of the fruit can be replaced by grapefruit (prepared like the orange), persimmon (wash but do not peel, and cut into pieces, passion fruit or granadilla (remove the stone and whisk together briefly with 2 tablespoons orange juice, using a hand-held mixer with whisk attachment) or pomegranate (cut open and remove the seeds). You need about 1 kg/2¼ lb fruit in all.

Raspberry
sorbet (photograph top)

Preparation time:
about 30 minutes,
excluding freezing time

150 ml/5 fl oz (⅝ cup) water
160 g/5½ oz sugar
peel of ½ lemon (untreated)
500 g/18 oz raspberries
2 teaspoons raspberry spirit

Per serving:
P: 2 g, F: 0 g, C: 46 g,
kJ: 877, kcal: 209

1 Add the sugar and lemon to the water in a small pan and bring to the boil and cook over high heat for about 5 minutes without a lid. This should produce about 100 ml/3½ fl oz (½ cup) syrup. Leave the syrup to cool down, then remove the lemon peel.

2 Sort out the raspberries but do not wash. Put the raspberries with half the syrup in a tall mixing glass and purée with a masher. Rub the mixture through a sieve if you like, add the rest of the syrup and flavour with raspberry spirit.

3 Put the mixture in a frost-resistant container and put in the freezer for 1 hour, stir and put back in the freezer for 3 hours, stirring several times to ensure a creamy texture.

4 Put the sorbet in a piping bag with a large star-shaped nozzle and squeeze into 4 individual bowls.

Tip: The sorbet can be made in an ice cream machine in 30–45 minutes, depending on the model.
200 ml/7 fl oz (⅞ cup) chilled whipped cream may be stirred into the fruit mixture before it is frozen.
Pour sparkling white wine over the sorbet in each bowl, 250 ml/8 fl oz (1 cup) in all.

Variation 1: Red currant sorbet. Use red currants instead of raspberries. Wash the red currants, drain thoroughly and remove from the stalks. Prepare the sorbet as described above, rub through a sieve and freeze.

Variation 2: Strawberry sorbet. Use strawberries instead of raspberries. Wash and drain the strawberries, remove the stalks and purée (do not rub through a sieve). Using only 100 g/3½ oz sugar for the syrup, prepare the sorbet as indicated above.

Variation 3: Mango sorbet (photograph bottom). For the syrup add 80 g/3 oz sugar, the peel of ½ lime (untreated) and 3 teaspoons lime juice to 125 ml/4 fl oz (½ cup) water and bring to the boil as indicated above (this will produce about 80 ml/3 fl oz syrup) and leave to cool. Remove the lime peel. Peel 2 mangoes, cut in half and remove the stones, cut the flesh into cubes and purée with a masher. Stir together the diced mangoes and the syrup and freeze for about 4 hours, stirring once or twice after the first hour. The sorbet may be crushed again with a masher just before serving or whisked with a hand-held mixer with whisk attachment.

Lemon pudding

Preparation time:
about 30 minutes,
excluding cooling time

4 leaves white gelatine
150 ml/5 fl oz (⅝ cup) lemon
juice, from about 3 lemons
125 g/4½ oz sugar
150 g/5 oz natural yogurt,
3.5% fat,
300 ml/10 fl oz (1¼ cups) chilled
whipping cream

Per serving:
P: 5 g, F: 25 g, C: 36 g,
kJ: 1669, kcal: 399

1 Soak the gelatine in cold water, following the instructions on the packet. Heat the lemon juice in a small pan but do not let it boil.

2 Squeeze the gelatine to remove some water, dissolve in the hot lemon juice, then stir in the sugar. Leave the gelatine and lemon mixture to cool down, then stir in the yogurt. Refrigerate the mixture until it begins to set, stirring occasionally.

3 When the mixture begins to set, whip the cream and fold in. Transfer this mixture into a glass bowl or individual bowls and refrigerate for at least 3 hours.

Tip: Serve the lemon pudding with whipped cream.

Variation 1: Serve the lemon pudding with chocolate sauce. To make the chocolate sauce, coarsely chop 100 g/3½ oz plain chocolate and melt with 3 tablespoons water in bowl placed in a bain-marie over low heat while stirring.

Variation 2: Orange pudding. Use freshly squeezed orange juice instead of lemon juice and use only 100 g/3½ oz sugar.

Vanilla sauce

Preparation time:
about 10 minutes,
excluding cooling time

1 vanilla pod
10 g/⅓ oz cornflour (cornstarch)
500 ml/17 fl oz (2¼ cups) milk
yolks of 3 large eggs
40 g/1½ oz sugar
1 pinch salt

Per serving:
P: 7 g, F: 9 g, C: 18 g,
kJ: 768, kcal: 183

1 Slit open the vanilla pod lengthways and scoop out the flesh with the back of a knife. Stir together the cornflour with 3 tablespoons of the milk, using a whisk. Then add the egg yolk, sugar and salt and stir well.

2 Bring the rest of the milk with the vanilla flesh to the boil. Remove the saucepan from the heat and stir in the mixture with the cornflour, using a whisk. Bring the sauce briefly to the boil.

3 Remove the sauce from the boil and leave to cool, stirring occasionally.

Tip: Vanilla sauce is delicious served with stewed fruit, red fruit pudding (page 154), baked apples (page 152) or apple pie.
100 ml/3½ fl oz (½ cup) of the milk may be replaced by whipping cream.

Bergische Waffeln

(Bergisch waffles, photograph, top)

Preparation and baking time:
about 60 minutes;

8–10 pieces

For the waffle iron:
some cooking oil

For the waffle mixture:
125 g/4½ oz (⅝ cup) soft
margarine or butter
75 g/3 oz (⅓ cup) sugar
2–3 drops vanilla essence
in 1 tablespoon sugar
2 medium eggs
250 g/9 oz (2½ cups) plain (all-
purpose) flour
½ level teaspoon baking powder
about 180 ml/6 oz buttermilk
4 teaspoons runny honey
some icing (confectioner's) sugar

Per piece:
P: 5 g, F: 13 g, C: 30 g,
kJ: 1095, kcal: 262

1 Preheat the waffle iron to the maximum setting.

2 To make the waffle mixture, stir the softened margarine or butter with a hand mixer with whisk until it becomes smooth and homogenous. Gradually add the sugar, vanilla sugar and salt and stir until the mixture thickens. Add 1 egg at a time, whisking each one for about ½ minute at the highest setting.

3 Mix together the baking powder and flour, sift and stir into the margarine or butter in two stages, alternating with the buttermilk, using the mixer at the medium setting. Finally stir in the honey.

4 Reduce the temperature of the waffle iron to medium and grease using a baking brush. Spoon the mixture onto the waffle iron in portions that are not too large. Bake until golden brown and leave to cool down (not stacked) on a rack. Dust the waffles with icing sugar.

Tip: Serve Bergisch waffles with sour cherries, rice pudding and cream.

Crème fraîche

waffles (photograph, middle)

Preparation and baking time:
about 60 minutes;

8–10 pieces

For the waffle iron:
some cooking oil

For the waffle mixture:
300 g/10 oz crème fraîche
100 g/3½ oz (½ cup) sugar
2–3 drops vanilla essence in
1 tablespoon sugar
grated zest of ½ untreated
lemon, 3 medium eggs
250 g/9 oz (2½ cups) plain (all-
purpose) flour
1 level teaspoon baking powder

Per piece:
P: 6 g, F: 13 g, C: 32 g,
kJ: 1119, kcal: 269

1 Preheat the waffle iron, at the highest setting.

2 To make the waffle mixture, whisk the crème fraîche briefly in a mixing bowl, using a hand mixer with whisk. Gradually add the sugar, vanilla sugar and grated lemon zest and stir until the mixture thickens. Add 1 egg at a time, whisking each one for about ½ minute at the highest setting.

3 Briefly mix together the flour and baking powder, sift and stir into the crème fraîche mixture in 2 stages, using the mixer at the medium setting.

4 Lower the waffle iron setting to medium and grease the waffle moulds. Spoon the mixture into the moulds in portions that are not too large and cook the waffles until golden brown. Leave to cool on a rack but do not stack them.

Baumkuchen (Layered cake)

Preparation and baking time:
about 80 minutes,
excluding cooling time;

about 20 pieces

For a rectangular tin
(30 x 11 cm/12 x 4½ in):
some fat
baking parchment

For the cake mixture:
whites of 4 medium eggs
250 g/9 oz (1¼ cups) soft
margarine or butter
250 g/9 oz (1⅛ cups) sugar
1 sachet vanilla sugar or 2–3
drops natural vanilla essence
in 1–2 tablespoons sugar
1 pinch salt
2 medium eggs
yolks of 4 medium eggs
4 tablespoons rum
150 g/6 oz (1½ cups) plain (all-
purpose) flour
100 g/4 oz (¾ cup) cornflour
(cornstarch)
3 level teaspoons baking powder

For the chocolate coating:
200 g/7 oz plain chocolate
4 teaspoons cooking oil

Per piece:
P: 4 g, F: 17 g, C: 27 g,
kJ: 1177, kcal: 281

1 Preheat the oven grill. Grease the rectangular tin and line the bottom with baking parchment.

2 To make the cake mixture, beat the egg whites until stiff. Stir the softened margarine or butter with a hand mixer with whisk until it becomes smooth and homogenous. Gradually add the sugar, vanilla sugar and salt, and stir until the mixture thickens. Add 1 egg at a time, whisking each one for about ½ minute at the highest setting. Then stir in the yolks and the rum.

3 Mix together the flour, cornflour and baking powder, sift and stir into the butter and egg mixture in two stages with the mixer set at the medium setting. Then carefully fold in the beaten egg whites using a flexible spatula or wooden spoon.

4 Using a brush, spread a heaped tablespoon of cake mixture on the bottom of the greased tin. Put the tin on a shelf in the oven (the dis-tance between the grill and the layer of cake mixture at the bottom of the tin should be about 20 cm/8 in). Grill for about 2 minutes under the preheated grill until golden brown.

5 Take the tin out of the oven and spread another layer (1–2 table-spoons of cake mixture) on top of the already baked layer. Put the tin under the grill again and continue in this way until all the cake mixture is used up. This means that the shelf on which the tin is placed will have to moved downwards to maintain a distance of 20 cm/8 in between the grill and the layer of cake mixture.

6 Carefully loosen the cake from the tin with a knife, remove from the tin and put on a rack. Remove the baking parchment and leave to cool.

7 To make the chocolate coating, finely chop the chocolate and melt with the oil in a bain-marie over low heat, stirring continuously. Then coat the cooled-down cake with the melted chocolate mixture.

Tip: To beat the egg whites very stiff, it is important that the bowl and whisk be completely fat-free and that the egg whites do not contain any trace of egg yolk.

Variation (photograph): To make Grillstangen, put a baking frame (25 x 25 cm/10 x 10 in) on a baking sheet lined with baking parchment. Use 1½ times the quantities given in the recipe above. Make the cake in layers as described above but with 3 tablespoons of cake mixture per

continued on page 168 ⫸

layer. The cake mixture can then be spread with a wide baking brush or cake slice. After baking, the baking frame can be loosened using a knife and removed. Remove the layered cake with the baking parchment from the baking sheet and place on a rack to cool down. Then cut the cake into six sticks 4 cm / 1½ in wide. Melt 300 g/10 oz plain chocolate with 2 tablespoons oil as described in the recipe above and coat the sticks with the melted chocolate. Wrap the sticks in aluminium foil so that they remain fresh, or freeze them.

Nut cake

Preparation time:
about 30 minutes,
excluding cooling time

Baking time:
about 50 minutes;

about 16 pieces

_____

For a loose-base springform tin (diameter 26 cm / 10 in):
some fat
plain (all-purpose) flour

For the cake mixture:
300 g/10 oz (1⅜ cups) soft margarine or butter
250 g/9 oz (1⅛ cups) sugar
5 drops vanilla essence in 1 tablespoon sugar
2 pinches ground cinnamon
6 medium eggs
180 g/7½ oz (2 cups) plain (all-purpose) flour
5 level teaspoons baking powder
400 g/14 oz ground hazelnut kernels

For the coating:
200 g/7 oz full milk chocolate
2 teaspoons cooking oil
50 g/2 oz plain chocolate

Per piece:
P: 8 g, F: 38 g, C: 36 g,
kJ: 2168, kcal: 518

1 Preheat the oven at the top and bottom. Grease and dust the tin.

2 To make the cake mixture, whisk the fat in a mixing bowl using a hand mixer with whisk until smooth and homogeneous. Gradually add the sugar, vanilla sugar and cinnamon and stir until the mixture thickens. Add 1 egg at a time, whisking each one for about ½ minute at the highest setting.

3 Mix together the flour and baking powder, sift and add the ground hazelnuts in 2 stages and stir briefly each time with the mixer at the medium setting. Put the cake mixture in the greased and floured tin. Put it on a shelf in the oven **for about 50 minutes**.

Top/bottom heat: about 180 °C/350 °F (preheated), Fan oven: about 160 °C/325 °F (not preheated), Gas mark 4 (not preheated).

4 Leave the cake in the tin for 10 minutes after taking it out of the oven, then remove from the tin and put on a rack to cool down.

5 To make the coating, coarsely chop the chocolate. Melt the milk chocolate with the oil and the plain chocolate separately in a bain-marie over low heat while stirring. Coat the cooled down cake with the melted milk chocolate, using a knife or baking brush. Sprinkle the melted plain chocolate on top using a teaspoon.

Variation: To make a Chocolate nut cake, use only 300 g/10 oz ground hazelnuts instead of 400 g/14 oz, and stir 100 g/3½ oz chopped chocolate into the cake mixture.

Frankfurter Kranz

Preparation time:
about 60 minutes,
excluding cooling time

Baking time:
about 40 minutes;

about 16 pieces

For a gugelhupf or ring mould
(diameter 22 cm/8½ in):
some fat
aluminium foil

For the cake mixture:
100 g/3½ oz (½ cup) soft
margarine or butter
150 g/5 oz (¾ cup) sugar
2–3 drops vanilla essence
in 1 tablespoon sugar
4 drops lemon essence
1 pinch salt
3 medium eggs
150 g/5 oz (1⅓ cups) plain (all-
purpose) flour
50 g/2 oz (½ cup) cornflour
(cornstarch)
2 level teaspoons baking powder

For the praline:
10 g/⅓ oz (2 teaspoons) butter
60 g/2 oz (¼ cup) sugar
125 g/4½ oz chopped blanched
almonds

For the butter cream:
40 g/1½ oz (4½ tablespoons)
custard powder, vanilla flavour
100 g/3½ oz (½ cup) sugar
500 ml/17 fl oz (2¼ cups) milk
250 g/9 oz soft butter

In addition:
2 tablespoons red currant jelly
or strawberry jam
some candied cherries

Per piece:
P: 5 g, F: 25 g, C: 33 g,
kJ: 1593, kcal: 380

1 Preheat the oven top and bottom. Grease the ring mould.

2 To make the cake mixture, stir the softened margarine or butter with a hand mixer with whisk until it becomes smooth and homogenous. Gradually add the sugar, vanilla sugar, flavouring and salt, and stir until the mixture thickens. Add 1 egg at a time, whisking each one for about ½ minute at the highest setting. Mix together the flour and baking powder, sift and stir briefly into the butter and egg mixture in 2 stages, using the mixer at the medium setting. Spoon the cake mixture into the ring mould, smooth out the surface and put on a shelf in the oven **for about 40 minutes**.

Top/bottom heat: about 180 °C/350 °F (preheated), Fan oven: about 160 °C/325 °F (not preheated), Gas mark 4 (not preheated).

3 Leave the cake in the mould for 10 minutes after taking it out of the oven, then remove from the tin and leave to cool. To make the praline, stir together the butter, sugar and almonds over low heat until the mixture turns brown, pour onto a piece of aluminium foil and leave to cool.

4 To make the butter cream, make the custard following the instructions on the tin but with 100 g/3½ oz (½ cup) sugar and milk. Let the custard cool (do not refrigerate), stirring occasionally. Whisk the softened butter with a hand mixer with whisk until smooth and homogeneous and stir into the cooled custard a spoonful at a time, making sure that the butter and custard are both at room temperature, or else it may curdle.

5 Whisk the jelly until it is smooth or rub the jam through a sieve. Cut the ring cake horizontally twice to make three layers and spread the jam or jelly on the bottom layer. Spread half the butter cream on the 2 lower layers, then put the top layer in place, thus reassembling the ring cake. Now coat the ring cake with the remaining butter cream (reserving 1–2 tablespoons) and sprinkle the praline all over the cake. Put the reserved butter cream in a piping bag with a star-shaped nozzle and decorate the cake. Finally, garnish with candied cherries. Refrigerate for about 2 hours.

Marble cake

Preparation time:
about 30 minutes

Baking time:
about 60 minutes;

about 20 pieces

For a gugelhupf mould
(diameter 24 cm/9½ in):
some fat

For the cake mixture:
300 g/10 oz (1⅜ cups) soft
margarine or butter
275 g/10 oz (1¼ cups) sugar
2–3 drops vanilla essence
in 1 tablespoon sugar
5–6 drops rum essence
1 pinch salt
5 medium eggs
375 g/13 oz (3¾ cups) plain (all-
purpose) flour
4 level teaspoons baking powder
about 2 tablespoons milk
20 g/¾ oz (2 tablespoons) cocoa
powder
20 g/¾ oz (2 tablespoons) sugar
1–2 tablespoons milk

For dusting:
some icing (confectioner's) sugar

Per piece:
P: 4 g, F: 15 g, C: 30 g,
kJ: 1135, kcal: 271

1 Preheat the oven at the top and bottom. Grease the mould.

2 To make the cake mixture, stir the softened fat with a hand mixer with whisk until it becomes smooth and homogenous. Gradually add the sugar, vanilla sugar, rum flavouring and salt, and stir until the mixture thickens. Add 1 egg at a time, whisking each one for about ½ minute at the highest setting.

3 Mix together the flour and baking powder, sift and add to the fat and egg mixture in 2 stages, alternating with the milk, stirring briefly with a mixer set at the medium setting.

4 Spoon two-thirds of the cake mixture into the greased gugelhupf. Sift the cocoa powder and add to the rest of the cake mixture together with the milk and sugar. Spoon the dark-coloured cake mixture on top of the light-coloured cake mixture and drag a fork through the two layers in a spiral movement to create a marbled pattern. Put the gugelhupf on a shelf in the oven **for about 60 minutes**.

Top/bottom heat: about 180 °C/350 °F (preheated), Fan oven: about 160 °C/325 °F (not preheated), Gas mark 4 (not preheated).

5 Leave the cake in the tin for 10 minutes after taking it out of the oven, then remove from the tin and leave on a rack to cool. Finally, dust with icing sugar.

Variation: Make the cake as shown in the illustration on the cover, using a well-greased rectangular tin (35 x 11 cm/14 x 4½ in). After about 15 minutes in the oven, make a cut about 1 cm/⅜ in deep in the middle along the length of the cake to ensure a neat crack in the centre and continue baking. Glaze with apricot jam after the cake has cooled down. Make the apricot glaze by rubbing 4 tablespoons apricot jam through a sieve and bringing the result to the boil with 1 tablespoon of water in a small pan. Use a brush to apply the glaze.

Lemon, cheese and cream torte

Preparation time:
about 35 minutes,
excluding cooling time

Baking time:
about 25 minutes;

about 16 pieces

For a springform tin
(diameter 28 cm/11 in):
some fat
baking parchment

For the cake mixture:
150 g/5 oz (¾ cup) soft
margarine or butter
150 g/5 oz (¾ cup) sugar
2-3 drops vanilla essence
in 1 tablespoon sugar
1 pinch salt
3 medium eggs
125 g/4½ oz (1¼ cups) plain
(all-purpose) flour
25 g/1 oz (3 tablespoons)
cornflour (cornstarch)
1 level teaspoon baking powder

For the filling:
12 sheets gelatine
500 ml/17 fl oz (2¼ cups) chilled
whipping cream
grated zest of 1 untreated lemon
100 ml/3½ fl oz (½ cup) lemon
juice
150 g/5 oz (¾ cup) sugar
2-3 drops vanilla essence
in 1 tablespoon sugar
500 g/18 oz curd cheese

For dusting:
25 g/1 oz (¼ cup) icing
(confectioner's) sugar

Per piece:
P: 11 g, F: 23 g, C: 33 g,
kJ: 1610, kcal: 384

1 Preheat the oven and grease the base of the springform tin.

2 To make the cake mixture, stir the softened margarine or butter with a hand mixer with whisk until it becomes smooth and homogenous. Gradually add the sugar, vanilla sugar and salt and stir until the mixture thickens.

3 Add 1 egg at a time, whisking each one for about ½ minute at the highest setting. Mix together the flour, cornflour and baking powder, sift and add to the margarine or butter and egg mixture in 2 stages, stirring briefly with a mixer on medium setting. Spoon the cake mixture into the springform tin, smooth the surface flat and put the mould on a shelf in the oven **for about 25 minutes**.

Top/bottom heat: about 180 °C/350 °F (preheated), Fan oven: about 160 °C/325 °F (preheated), Gas mark 4 (preheated).

4 Remove the cake from the oven, leave to cool down and cut in half horizontally.

5 To make the filling, soak the gelatine following the instructions on the packet. In the meantime, whisk the cream until it is stiff. Then add the lemon zest, lemon juice, sugar and vanilla sugar to the curd cheese and mix well.

6 Dissolve the gelatine and first add 4 tablespoons of the curd cheese mixture. Then stir in the rest of the quark mixture. Carefully fold in the whipped cream. Place the ring part of the springform tin, lined with baking parchment, round the bottom layer, spread the quark and cream mixture on top and smooth the surface flat.

7 Cut the top layer into 16 slices. Put them on top of the filling and refrigerate the torte for at least 3 hours. Loosen the torte with a knife, remove the springform tin ring and dust with icing sugar.

Tip: You can make the cake even fruitier by adding a tin of mandarins (drained weight 175 g/6 oz). Drain thoroughly in a sieve and fold into the cream cheese mixture using a spatula or dough scraper.

Maulwurftorte ("Mole cake")

Preparation time:
about 30 minutes,
excluding cooling time

Baking time:
about 30 minutes;

about 16 pieces

For a springform tin
(diameter 26 cm / 10 in):
some fat

For the cake mixture:
whites of 4 medium eggs
125 g / 4½ oz (⅝ cup) soft
margarine or butter
125 g / 4½ oz (⅝ cup) sugar
3 drops vanilla essence
in 1 tablespoon sugar
yolks of 4 medium eggs
50 g / 2 oz (½ cup) plain (all-
purpose) flour
10 g / ⅓ oz cocoa powder
4 level teaspoons baking powder
75 g / 3 oz ground hazelnut
kernels
100 g / 3½ oz grated dark bitter
chocolate

For the filling:
1 can or jar sour cherries
(drained weight 350 g / 12 oz)
2 bananas (250 g / 9 oz)
4 teaspoons lemon juice
600 ml / 21 oz (2½ cups) chilled
whipping cream
25 g / 1 oz (2 tablespoons) sugar
3 drops vanilla essence
in 1 tablespoon sugar

Per piece:
P: 5 g, F: 25 g, C: 26 g,
kJ: 1450, kcal: 346

1 Preheat the oven and grease the base of the springform tin.

2 To make the cake mixture, beat the egg whites very stiff. Stir the softened fat with a hand mixer with whisk until it becomes smooth and homogenous. Gradually add the sugar and vanilla sugar, stir until the mixture has thickened. Add the egg yolks one at a time, whisking with the mixer at the highest setting.

3 Mix together the cocoa powder and baking powder, sift, add the hazelnuts and grated chocolate to the fat and egg mixture in 2 stages and stir briefly using a mixer at the medium setting. Briefly whisk in the beaten egg whites using a mixer on medium setting. Put the cake mixture in the springform tin and smooth the surface flat. Put the tin on a shelf in the oven **for about 30 minutes**.

Top/bottom heat: about 180 °C/350 °F (preheated), Fan oven: about 160 °C/325 °F (preheated), Gas mark 4 (preheated).

4 Leave the cake in the tin for about 10 minutes after taking it out of the oven. Then remove it from the tin and put on a rack to cool. When cool, scoop out the cake with a spoon to a depth of 1 cm/⅜ in, leaving a rim of about 1–2 cm/⅜–¾ in (photograph 1). To ensure a neat rim, cut round the cake with the tip of a knife before scooping out the middle. Crumble the scooped out cake in a bowl (photograph 2).

5 For the filling, drain the cherries thoroughly in a colander, then put on kitchen paper. Peel the bananas, cut in half lengthways, sprinkle with lemon juice and arrange in the scooped out cake. Then arrange the cherries on top. Whip the cream with sugar and vanilla sugar, spoon on the fruit to form a dome (photograph 3) and sprinkle with the crumbled cake. Refrigerate for 1 hour.

Lemon cake

Preparation time:
about 35 minutes

Baking time:
about 25 minutes;

about 20 pieces

For a baking sheet
(40 x 30 cm/16 x 12 in)
or roasting tin:
some fat
plain (all-purpose) flour
aluminium foil

For the cake mixture:
350 g/12 oz (1¾ cups) soft
margarine or butter
350 g/12 oz (1¾ cups) sugar
grated zest of 2 untreated
lemons
5 medium eggs
275 g/9½ oz (2¾ cups) plain
(all-purpose) flour
120 g/4½ oz (1 cup) cornflour
(cornstarch)
2 level teaspoons baking powder

For the icing:
250 g/9 oz (1¾ cups) icing
(confectioner's) sugar
about 5 tablespoons lemon juice

Per piece:
P: 3 g, F: 16 g, C: 46 g,
kJ: 1450, kcal: 346

1 Preheat the oven. Grease and flour the baking sheet or roasting tin.

2 To make the cake mixture, stir the softened margarine or butter with a hand mixer with whisk until it becomes smooth and homogenous. Gradually add the sugar and lemon zest and stir until the mixture thickens. Add 1 egg at a time, whisking each one for about ½ minute at the highest setting.

3 Mix together the plain (all-purpose) flour and baking powder, sift and add to margarine or butter and egg mixture in two stages, briefly stirring with a mixer at the medium setting. Spread the cake mixture on the greased and floured baking sheet or roasting tray and smooth the surface flat.

4 Place a strip of aluminium foil along the open end of the baking sheet to form an edge and put the baking sheet in the oven **for about 25 minutes**.

Top/bottom heat: about 180 °C/350 °F (preheated), Fan oven: about 160 °C/325 °F (preheated), Gas mark 4 (preheated).

5 For the icing, sift the icing sugar and stir in enough lemon juice to obtain a smooth, thick mixture. Put the baking sheet or roasting tray on a rack and coat the cake – while still hot – with the icing (the hotter the cake, the more the icing will penetrate the cake). Leave the cake to cool on the baking sheet or roasting tray, placed on a rack.

Variation: To make orange cake, use orange zest instead of lemon zest.

Fruit tart

Preparation time:
about 25 minutes,
excluding cooling time

Baking time:
about 15 minutes;

about 12 pieces

For a deep flan tin (diameter
28 or 30 cm/11 or 12 in)
or 6 tartlet moulds (diameter
12 cm/5 in):
some fat

For the all-in-one mixture:
125 g/4½ oz (1¼ cups) plain
(all-purpose) flour
2½ level teaspoons baking
powder
100 g/3½ oz (½ cup) sugar
3 drops vanilla essence
in 1 tablespoon sugar
4 medium eggs
2 tablespoons cooking oil,
e.g. sunflower oil
4 teaspoons vinegar, e.g. fruit
vinegar

For the filling:
about 1 kg/2¼ lb fresh fruit
(e.g. strawberries, oranges,
bananas, grapes, kiwi fruit)
some sugar

For the glaze:
2 teaspoons arrowroot
4 teaspoons sugar
250 ml/8 fl oz (1 cup) water

Per piece:
P: 4 g, F: 5 g, C: 35 g,
kJ: 865, kcal: 206

1 Preheat the oven. Grease the flan tin or tartlet moulds.

2 To make the cake mixture, mix together the flour and baking powder, sift into a mixing bowl, add the other ingredients one after the
other, stir with a hand mixer, first briefly at the lowest setting, then for
2 minutes at the highest setting, to obtain a smooth consistency.

3 Put the mixture in the greased flan dish or tartlet tin, smooth the
surface flat and put it on the lowest shelf in the oven **for about
15 minutes**.

Top/bottom heat: about 200 °C/400 °F (preheated), Fan oven: about
180 °C/350 °F (preheated), Gas mark 6 (preheated).

4 After removing from the oven, put the flan case on a rack lined with
baking parchment and leave to cool.

5 To make the filling, peel or wash the fruit, drain well, remove the
stalks and cut in half or slices if necessary. Sprinkle the fruit with sugar
and leave to stand for a short time. Arrange the fruit in the flan case
or tartlet cases.

6 To make the arrowroot glaze, take 250 ml/8 fl oz (1 cup) water
or fruit juice. Blend 2 teaspoons arrowroot with a little of the liquid,
then stir in the rest of the liquid. Bring to the boil and simmer for
½–1 minute until it is clear. When cool, pour it over the fruit using a
tablespoon. Leave the glaze to set before serving.

Tips: If you use a tin flan dish, grease and flour it first.
Instead of fresh fruit, tinned fruit to choice (drained weight about
500 g/18 oz) can be used. Drain the fruit thoroughly, reserve the juice
and use to make the glaze.

Quick plum cake

Preparation time:
about 35 minutes

Baking time:
about 50 minutes;

about 12 pieces

For a springform tin
(diameter 26 cm/10 in):
some fat

For the filling:
800 g/1¾ lb plums

For the all-in-one mixture:
125 g/4½ oz (1¼ cup) plain (all-purpose) flour
1 level teaspoons baking powder
125 g/4½ oz (⅝ cup) sugar
3 drops vanilla essence
in 1 tablespoon sugar
grated zest of 1 untreated lemon
125 g/4½ oz (⅝ cup) soft butter
or margarine
2 medium eggs

For the crumble:
150 g/5 oz (1⅓ cup) plain (all-purpose) flour
100 g/3½ oz (½ cup) sugar
1 pinch ground cinnamon
100 g/3½ oz (½ cup) soft butter

Per piece:
P: 4 g, F: 17 g, C: 42 g,
kJ: 1407, kcal: 336

1 Preheat the oven at the top and bottom. Grease the base of the springform tin. For the filling, wash the plums, pat dry, remove the stones and cut lengthways from the top.

2 To make the cake mixture, mix together the flour and baking powder, sift into a mixing bowl, add the other ingredients and stir with a hand mixer, first briefly at the lowest setting, then for 2 minutes at the highest setting, to obtain a smooth consistency.

3 Spoon the mixture into the springform tin and smooth the surface flat. Arrange the plums on the mixture so that they overlap, with the hollow side upward.

4 To make the crumble, sift the plain flour in a mixing bowl, add the cinnamon, sugar and softened butter. Whisk until the crumble has the right texture. Sprinkle the crumble over the plums and put on a shelf in the oven **for about 50 minutes**.

Top/bottom heat: about 180 °C/350 °F (preheated), Fan oven: about 160 °C/325 °F (not preheated), Gas mark 4 (not preheated).

5 Take the cake out of the springform tin and put on a rack to cool down.

Tip: This cake can also be made with apples instead of plums. Use 800 g/1¾ lb apples such as Elstar or Jonagold. Wash, peel and core them, then cut into slices.

Raspberry and yogurt cake

Preparation time:
about 40 minutes,
excluding cooling time

Baking time:
about 15 minutes;

about 12 pieces

For the baking sheet:
some fat
baking parchment
baking frame

For the all-in-one mixture:
125 g/4½ oz (1¼ cups) plain (all-purpose) flour
25 g/1 oz (3 tablespoons) cornflour (cornstarch)
1 heaped teaspoon cocoa powder
3 heaped teaspoons baking powder
100 g/3½ oz (½ cup) sugar
3 drops vanilla essence in 1 tablespoon sugar
60 g/2 oz (4 tablespoons) soft butter or margarine
3 medium eggs

For the topping:
10–12 sheets gelatine
1 untreated lime
1 kg/2¼ lb yogurt
150 g/5 oz (¾ cup) sugar
3 drops vanilla essence in 1 tablespoon sugar
400 ml/14 fl oz (1¾ cups) chilled whipping cream
250 g/9 oz raspberries
60 g/2 oz raspberry jelly

Per piece:
P: 8 g, F: 19 g, C: 41 g,
kJ: 1560, kcal: 373

1 Grease the baking sheet and line with baking parchment. Place a baking frame (30 x 40 cm/12 x 16 in) on the baking sheet.

2 To make the cake mixture, mix together the flour and cornflour, cocoa powder and baking powder and sift into a mixing bowl, add the other ingredients and stir with a mixer, first briefly at the lowest setting, then for 2 minutes at the highest setting, to obtain a smooth consistency.

3 Spread the mixture in the baking frame on the baking sheet, smooth the surface flat and put in the oven **for about 15 minutes**.

Top/bottom heat: about 200 °C/400 °F (preheated), Fan oven: about 180 °C/350 °F (preheated), Gas mark: 6 (preheated).

4 Loosen the baking frame with a knife and remove it. Put the cake on a rack, lined with baking parchment, to cool down. Wash the baking frame. Carefully peel the baking parchment off the cake. Put the cake on a plate and enclose it again with the baking frame.

5 To make the topping, soak the gelatine following the instructions on the packet. Wash the limes in hot water and wipe dry. Grate the lime zest with a lemon zester and press the juice from the lime. Stir together the yogurt, sugar, vanilla sugar, lime zest and lime juice. Squeeze out the gelatine and dissolve. First whisk 4 tablespoons of the yogurt mixture into the dissolved gelatine, then whisk in the rest of the yogurt mixture.

6 When the yogurt and gelatine mixture begins to thicken, whip the cream, fold into the mixture and spread this mixture on the cake. Clean and prepare the raspberries and scatter over the topping. Refrigerate the cake for about 3 hours.

7 Bring the raspberry jelly to the boil in a small pan. While still hot, pour it in blobs or thin streaks over the cake and allow to set. Then carefully loosen and remove the baking frame.

Tip: Garnish the cake with lemon balm leaves if desired.

Nut triangles

1 Preheat the oven and grease the baking sheet.

2 To make the dough, mix together the flour and baking powder, sift into a mixing bowl and add the other ingredients. Stir with a hand mixer with kneading hook, first briefly at the lowest setting, then at the highest setting until the dough is formed. Then roll it into a cylinder using your hands. Roll out the dough on the greased baking sheet.

3 For the topping, spread the jam on the dough (photograph 1). Melt the butter together with the sugar, vanilla sugar and water in a pan, stirring continuously. Add the ground and flaked hazelnut kernels to the mixture and stir well. Leave the mixture to cool down a little and spread evenly over the dough (photograph 2). Put a piece of aluminium foil for the dough to make an edge. Put the baking sheet in the oven **for about 25 minutes.**

Top/bottom heat: about 180 °C/350 °F (preheated), Fan oven: about 160 °C/325 °F (preheated), Gas mark 4 (preheated).

4 Leave the biscuits to cool down on the baking sheet placed on a wire rack. Cut into squares (4 x 4 cm/2½ x 2½ in) and then cut diagonally into triangles (photograph 3).

5 To make the coating, coarsely chop the chocolate and melt in a bain-marie over low heat while stirring. Dip the two pointed corners of the triangles into the melted chocolate and allow to set.

Preparation time:
about 30 minutes, excluding cooling time

Baking time:
about 25 minutes;

about 140 pieces

For a baking sheet
(40 x 30 cm/16 x 12 in):
some fat
aluminium foil

For the shortcrust pastry:
225 g/8 oz (2¼ cups) plain (all-purpose) flour
1 level teaspoon baking powder
100 g/3½ oz (½ cup) sugar
3 drops vanilla essence
in 1 tablespoon sugar
1 medium egg
yolk of 1 medium egg
100 g/3½ oz (⅜ cup) soft butter or margarine

For the topping:
2 tablespoons apricot preserve
150 g/5 oz (¾ cup) butter
150 g/5 oz (¾ cup) sugar
6 drops vanilla essence
in 1 tablespoon sugar
2 tablespoons water
100 g/3½ oz ground hazelnut kernels
200 g/7 oz flaked hazelnut kernels

For the coating:
200 g/7 oz plain chocolate

Per piece:
P: 1 g, F: 3 g, C: 4 g,
kJ: 204, kcal: 49

Tips: Instead of the dipping the corners of the triangles in the melted chocolate, you can spatter the triangles with the melted chocolate after cutting up. But then use only 100 g/3½ oz chocolate.
Stored in air-tight container, the biscuits will keep for about 2 weeks.

Leipziger Lerchen

(typical Saxon speciality)

Preparation time:
about 30 minutes

Baking time:
about 25 minutes;

12 pieces

For 12 moulds (bottom diameter about 4 cm/1½ in, top about 8 cm/3 in, depth 3–4 cm/1¼–1½ in):
some fat

For the shortcrust pastry:
200 g/7 oz (2 cups) plain (all-purpose) flour
½ level teaspoon baking powder
75 g/2½ oz (⅜ cup) sugar
3 drops vanilla essence in 1 tablespoon sugar
1 pinch salt
4 teaspoons water
100 g/3½ oz (½ cup) soft butter or margarine

100 g/3½ oz apricot preserve

For the filling:
80 g/3 oz (generous ⅜ cup) soft butter
125 g/4½ oz (⅝ cup) sugar
1 pinch salt, 1 medium egg
white of 1 medium egg
100 g/3½ oz (1 cup) plain (all-purpose) flour
125 g/4½ oz blanched ground almonds
1 drop almond essence
3 tablespoons milk
4 teaspoons rum

For the spread:
yolk of 1 medium egg
1 teaspoon milk

Per piece:
P: 6 g, F: 20 g, C: 41 g,
kJ: 1547, kcal: 370

1 Preheat the oven and grease the small fluted moulds.

2 To make the dough, mix together the flour and baking powder, sift into a mixing bowl, add the other ingredients and stir with a hand mixer with kneading hook, first briefly at the lowest setting, then at the highest setting until the dough is formed. Then roll it into a ball using your hands.

3 Roll out the dough thinly and cut out 12 circles (diameter about 10 cm/4 in) (photograph 1) and line the greased moulds with it. Using the rest of the dough, cut out 12 small stars and put to one side. Now put 1 tablespoonful jam in each of the moulds (photograph 2).

4 To make the filling, stir the softened butter in a mixing bowl to obtain a smooth consistency, using a hand mixer. Add the sugar, salt, egg and egg white and stir well. Sift the flour and add with the almonds, almond essence, milk and rum to the butter mixture and stir well. Put this mixture in the moulds and decorate each with a star (photograph 3). Beat together the egg yolk and milk and coat the stars with it. Place the moulds on a shelf in the oven **for about 25 minutes**.

Top/bottom heat: about 180 °C/350 °F (preheated), Fan oven: about 160 °C/325 °F (preheated), Gas mark 4 (preheated).

5 Leave the tartlets in the moulds for 10 minutes, then take out of the moulds and put on a wire rack to cool down.

Berliner Bobbes

(typical Berlin speciality)

Preparation time:
about 45 minutes,
excluding cooling time

Baking time:
about 15 minutes;

about 20 pieces

For the baking sheet:
baking parchment
For the shortcrust pastry:
375 g/13½ oz (3¾ cups) plain
(all-purpose) flour
40 g/1½ oz (5 tablespoons)
cornflour (cornstarch)
1 level teaspoon baking powder
150 g/5 oz (¾ cup) sugar
3 drops vanilla essence
in 1 tablespoon sugar
2 drops lemon essence
3 yolks of medium eggs
250 g/9 oz (1¼ cups) soft butter
1 pinch salt

For the filling:
100 g/3½ oz blanched chopped
almonds
200 g/7 oz marzipan
60 g/2 oz (¼ cup) sugar
100 ml/3½ fl oz (½ cup) rum
100 g/3½ oz sultanas
100 g/3½ oz candied orange
peel

For the crumble:
75 g/2½ oz (¾ cup) plain (all-
purpose) flour
25 g/1 oz (2 tablespoons) sugar
1 pinch ground cinnamon
50 g/2 oz (4 tablespoons) soft
butter

white of 1 medium egg
icing (confectioner's) sugar

Per piece:
P: 5 g, F: 20 g, C: 40 g,
kJ: 1564, kcal: 374

1 To make the dough, mix together the flour and baking powder, sift into a mixing bowl, add the other ingredients and stir with a hand mixer with kneading hook, first briefly at the lowest setting, then at the highest setting until the dough is formed. Then roll it into a ball using your hands. Wrap the dough in clingfilm and refrigerate for about 30 minutes.

2 To make the filling, roast the almonds in a pan without fat until golden brown and put on a plate to cool down. Cut the marzipan finely, put in a mixing bowl, add the sugar and rum and stir with a hand mixer with whisk until the mixture has become easy to spread.

3 Divide the dough in half. Roll each half on a floured work top to make a rectangle 35 x 30 cm (14 x 12 in) and cover with the marzipan mixture. Sprinkle the sultanas, roast almonds and candied orange peel on top. Roll up the dough loosely, starting with the longer edge, and refrigerate the rolls for about 20–30 minutes. Meanwhile, preheat the oven and line the baking sheet with baking parchment.

4 To make the crumble, sift the flour into a mixing bowl, add the sugar, cinnamon and softened butter and whisk with a hand mixer with whisk until the crumble has the right consistency. Coat the rolls with egg white and sprinkle the crumble on top. Press the crumble down lightly. Cut each roll into 10 pieces each 3.5 cm/1⅜ in wide and put upright on the baking sheet lined with baking parchment. Put the baking sheet in the oven **for about 15 minutes**.

Top/bottom heat: about 200 °C/400 °F (preheated), Fan oven: about 180 °C/350 °F (preheated), Gas mark 6 (preheated).

5 Put the baking sheet on wire rack and leave the pastries to cool. Dust with icing sugar before serving.

Tip: Berliner Bobbes will keep fresh for 3–4 days in an airtight container.

Cheesecake with crumble

Preparation time:
about 40 minutes,
excluding cooling time

Baking time:
about 85 minutes;

about 12 pieces

For a springform tin
(diameter 28 cm/11 in):
some fat

For the shortcrust pastry:
150 g/5 oz (1⅓ cup) plain (all-purpose) flour
½ level teaspoon baking powder
75 g/2½ oz (⅜ cup) sugar
3 drops vanilla essence
in 1 tablespoon sugar
1 pinch salt
1 medium egg
75 g/2½ oz (⅜ cup) soft butter
or margarine

For the filling:
whites of 3 medium eggs
250 ml/8 fl oz (1 cup) chilled
whipping cream
750 g/1½ lb curd cheese (low fat)
150 g/5 oz (¾ cup) sugar
2 tablespoons lemon juice
50 g/2 oz (6 tablespoons)
cornflour (cornstarch)
yolks of 3 medium eggs

For the crumble:
100 g/3½ oz (1 cup) plain (all-purpose) flour
75 g/2½ oz (⅜ cup) sugar
3 drops vanilla essence
in 1 tablespoon sugar
75 g/2½ oz (⅜ cup) soft butter
or margarine

Per piece:
P: 14 g, F: 19 g, C: 48 g,
kJ: 1771, kcal: 423

1 Preheat the oven and grease the base of the springform tin.

2 To make the dough, mix together the flour and baking powder, sift into a mixing bowl and add the other ingredients. Stir with a hand mixer with kneading hook, first briefly at the lowest setting, then at the highest setting until the dough is formed. Then roll it into a ball using your hands. Roll out two-thirds of the dough, line the greased base of the springform tin with it and put the ring back round the base. Prick the base several times, put the mould on a shelf in the oven and pre-bake the case **for about 10 minutes**.

Top/bottom heat: about 200 °C/400 °F (preheated), Fan oven: about 180 °C/350 °F (preheated), Gas mark 6 (preheated).

3 After removing from the oven put the springform tin on a rack and let the cheesecake base cool down a little. Roll the rest of the dough into a long cylinder and place around the base, pressing lightly against the sides to form an edge 3 cm/1¼ in high.

4 To make the filling, first beat the egg whites until they are very stiff, then whip the cream until stiff. Mix together the curd cheese, sugar, lemon juice, cornflour and egg yolk. Now fold the stiffly beaten egg whites and whipped cream into the cream cheese mixture and spread this mixture evenly over the cheesecake base.

5 To make the crumble, sift the plain (all-purpose) flour in a mixing bowl, add the other ingredients and stir with a hand mixer with whisk to make the crumble. Sprinkle the crumble evenly over the filling. Put the springform tin on a shelf in the oven and continue baking but at a lower temperature **for about 75 minutes**.

Top/bottom heat: about 160 °C/325 °F (preheated),
Fan oven: about 140 °C/285 °F (preheated), Gas mark 3 (preheated).

6 When done, turn off the oven but leave the cheesecake inside with the door slightly open for another 15 minutes to prevent the top from cracking. Then put the cheesecake on rack to cool down but without removing it from the mould.

Variation: To make a traditional cheesecake (photograph, top) leave out the crumble.

Friesische Streuseltorte

(Friesian crumble torte)

Preparation time:
about 50 minutes,
excluding cooling time

Baking time:
15 minutes per layer;

about 12 pieces

For a springform tin
(diameter 28 cm/11 in):
some fat

For the shortcrust pastry:
250 g/9 oz (2½ cups) plain (all-purpose) flour
1 pinch baking powder
6 drops vanilla essence
in 3 tablespoons sugar
150 g/5 oz crème fraîche
175 g/6 oz (⅞ cup) soft butter
or margarine

For the crumble:
150 g/5 oz (1⅓ cup) plain (all-purpose) flour
75 g/2½ oz (⅜ cup) sugar
3 drops vanilla essence
in 1 tablespoon sugar
1 pinch ground cinnamon
100 g/3½ oz (½ cup) soft butter
or margarine

For the filling:
500 ml/17 fl oz (2¼ cups) chilled
whipping cream
25 g/1 oz (2 tablespoons) sugar
3 drops vanilla essence
in 1 tablespoon sugar
450 g/16 oz plum purée

icing (confectioner's) sugar

Per piece:
P: 5 g, F: 36 g, C: 55 g,
kJ: 2336, kcal: 558

1 Prepare the oven and grease the base of the springform tin.

2 To make the dough, mix together the flour and baking powder, sift into a mixing bowl, add the other ingredients for the dough. Stir with a hand mixer with kneading hook, first briefly at the lowest setting, then at the highest setting until the dough is formed. Then divide the dough into 4 equal portions and shape into balls using your hands. Roll out one portion evenly and line the base of the springform tin, prick several times with a fork and put the ring of the springform tin back round the base.

3 To make the crumble, sift the flour into a mixing bowl and add the other ingredients. Add the softened butter and stir with a hand mixer with whisk to make a crumble. Sprinkle a quarter of the crumble on the dough base (photograph 1) and put the springform tin in the oven **for about 15 minutes.** Make the other three layers in the same way and bake.

Top/bottom heat: about 200 °C/400 °F (preheated), Fan oven: about 180 °C/350 °F (preheated), Gas mark 6 (preheated).

4 Remove the cake layers immediately from the springform tin, cut one of the layers into 12 slices while still warm and leave the layers to cool on a rack, not stacked on each other.

5 To make the filling, beat the whipping cream with the sugar and vanilla sugar until stiff. Put a small amount at a time into a piping bag with a star-shaped nozzle (diameter 8 mm/⅓ in). Cover each of the 3 unsliced layers with one-third of the plum purée, pipe one-third of the whipped cream around it (photograph 2) and assemble to make the torte, placing the sliced layer on top (photograph 3). Refrigerate the torte for about 1 hour and dust with icing sugar just before serving if desired.

Cherry crumble cake

Preparation time:
about 60 minutes,
excluding cooling time

Baking time:
about 52 minutes;

about 12 pieces

For a springform tin
(diameter 26 cm/10 in):
some fat

For the shortcrust pastry:
150 g/5 oz (1⅓ cup) plain (all-purpose) flour
1 pinch baking powder
100 g/3½ oz (½ cup) sugar
3 drops vanilla essence
in 1 tablespoon sugar
1 pinch salt
1 medium egg
100 g/3½ oz (⅜ cup) soft butter
or margarine

For the filling:
1 kg/2¼ lb sour cherries
100 g/3½ oz (½ cup) sugar
20 g/1 oz (2 tablespoons)
cornflour (cornstarch)
about 2 teaspoons sugar

For the crumble:
150 g/5 oz (1⅓ cup) plain (all-purpose) flour
100 g/3½ oz (½ cup) sugar
3 drops vanilla essence
in 1 tablespoon sugar
100 g/3½ oz (⅜ cup) soft butter
or margarine

Per piece:
P: 4 g, F: 15 g, C: 55 g,
kJ: 1565, kcal: 374

1 To make the dough, mix together the flour and baking powder, sift into a mixing bowl and add the other ingredients. Stir with a hand mixer with kneading hook, first briefly at the lowest setting, then at the highest setting until the dough is formed. Then roll it into a ball using your hands. Wrap in clingfilm and refrigerate for about 20–30 minutes.

2 Meanwhile, preheat the oven and grease the base of the springform tin. Wash the cherries, drain, remove the stalks and stones. Stir in the sugar, mix well and let stand for a while for the sugar to draw the juice.

3 Roll out two-thirds of the dough and line the greased base of the springform tin. Prick here and there with a fork and put the ring of the springform tin back around the base. Put the springform tin on a shelf in the oven and pre-bake **for about 12 minutes.**

Top/bottom heat: about 200 °C/400 °F (preheated), Fan oven: about 180 °C/350 °F (preheated), Gas mark 6 (preheated).

4 Put the springform tin on a wire rack and let the pastry base cool down a little.

5 Bring the cherries in their juice to the boil briefly in a pan, drain in a sieve, collect the juice and reserve 250 ml/8 fl oz (1 cup) of it, making up the quantity with water if necessary. Stir 4 tablespoons of this juice into the cornflour. Bring the rest of the juice to the boil, add the cornflour and juice mixture to the juice and bring back to the boil briefly. Stir in the cherries and add sugar to taste.

6 Shape the rest of the dough into a long cylinder and place round the base to form an edge, pressing it lightly against the side of the springform tin until it is about 2 cm/¾ in high. Now put the cherries on the pastry base.

7 To make the crumble, sift the flour in a mixing bowl and add the other ingredients for the crumble. Mix all the ingredients together with a hand mixer with whisk to make a crumble of the right consistency and spread over the cherries. Return the cake to the oven and bake at the same temperature **for about 40 minutes until done.**

8 Leave the cake in the mould for about 15 minutes. Then loosen the edges of the pie with a knife and carefully remove the ring. Loosen the base of the pie to detach it from the base of the springform tin but leaving it on it. Put on a wire rack to cool down, still on the springform tin base.

Angels' eyes

Preparation time:
about 40 minutes,
excluding cooling time

Baking time:
about 15 minutes
per baking sheet;

about 140 pieces/
3 baking sheets

For the baking sheet:
baking parchment

For the shortcrust pastry:
250 g/9 oz (2½ cups) plain (all-purpose) flour
1 level teaspoon baking powder
100 g/3½ oz (½ cup) sugar
3 drops vanilla essence
in 1 tablespoon sugar
1 pinch salt
yolks of 3 medium eggs
150 g/5 oz (¾ cup) soft butter
or margarine

In addition:
whites of 2 medium eggs
75 g/2½ oz blanched chopped
almonds
4 tablespoons redcurrant
or other jelly
2 teaspoons water

Per piece:
P: 1 g, F: 1 g, C: 2 g,
kJ: 97, kcal: 23

1 To make the dough, mix together the flour and baking powder, sift into a mixing bowl, add the other ingredients and stir with a hand mixer with kneading hook, first briefly at the lowest setting, then at the highest setting until the dough is formed. Then form it into a ball using your hands. Wrap the dough in clingfilm and put in the refrigerator for 30 minutes.

2 Meanwhile preheat the oven and line the baking sheet with baking parchment.

3 Mould the dough into 7 cylinders (40 cm/16 in long), cut into pieces 2 cm/¾ in long and then form them into small balls.

4 Whisk the egg whites with a fork. Dip one side of each ball of dough in the beaten egg white, then press into the chopped almonds. Then place the balls of dough with the non-almond side downwards on the baking sheet and make a hollow in each ball of dough using the handle of a wooden spoon. Put the baking sheet in the oven **for about 15 minutes**.

Top/bottom heat: about 180 °C/350 °F (preheated), Fan oven: about 160 °C/325 °F (preheated), Gas mark 4 (preheated).

5 When the biscuits are done, remove from the baking sheet with the baking parchment and put on a rack (with the baking parchment) to cool down.

6 Bring the jelly with water to the boil and fill the hollowed centre of the biscuits using a teaspoon.

Tip: Redcurrant or raspberry jelly are the most suitable for the purpose. But yellow jam can also be used, which should first be rubbed through a sieve.
If the jelly begins to set again, warm it up once more.

Covered apple pie

Preparation time:
about 50 minutes,
excluding cooling time

Baking time:
about 25 minutes;

about 20 pieces

For a baking sheet
(40 x 30 cm / 16 x 12 in):
some fat

For the filling:
1.5 kg/3¼ lb apples
50 g/1¾ oz (4 tablespoons) sugar
3 drops vanilla essence in 1 tablespoon sugar
1 pinch ground cinnamon
30 g/1 oz raisins
50 g/1¾ oz (4 tablespoons) butter
about 50 g/1¾ oz (4 tablespoons) sugar

For the shortcrust pastry:
400 g/14 oz (4 cups) plain (all-purpose) flour
4 level teaspoons baking powder
70 g/2½ oz (⅜ cup) sugar
3 drops vanilla essence in 1 tablespoon sugar
2 medium eggs
3 tablespoons milk
150 g/5 oz (¾ cup) soft butter or margarine

For the coating:
yolk of 1 medium egg
2 teaspoons milk
50 g/2 oz blanched flaked almonds

Per piece:
P: 4 g, F: 11 g, C: 33 g,
kJ: 1040, kcal: 249

1 Preheat the oven and grease the baking sheet.

2 To make the apple filling, wash the apples, peel, quarter and core them and cut into sticks or small pieces. Lightly braise the apples together with the sugar, vanilla sugar and butter in a pan while stirring. Leave to cool and season with sugar.

3 To make the dough, mix together the flour and baking powder, sift into a mixing bowl and add the other ingredients. Stir with a hand mixer with kneading hook, first briefly at the lowest setting, then at the highest setting until the dough is formed. Then roll it into a cylinder using your hands.

4 Roll out half the dough thinly to the same size as the baking sheet. Place a piece of paper of similar size on top and carefully roll up together (photograph 1). Roll out the rest of the dough to line the greased baking sheet (photograph 2). Spread the apple filling on top and unroll the piece of dough and cover (photograph 3).

5 Beat together the egg yolk and milk, brush over the lid and scatter the flaked almonds on top. Carefully prick the lid here and there with a fork and put in the oven **for about 25 minutes**.

Top/bottom heat: about 200 °C/400 °F (preheated), Fan oven: about 180 °C/350 °F (preheated), Gas mark 6 (preheated).

Tip: The cake can also be baked in a springform tin (diameter 26 cm/ 10 in), in which case the quantities of dough and filling are halved.

Custard snails

Preparation time:
about 50 minutes,
excluding rising time

Baking time:
about 15 minutes
per baking sheet;

about 20 pieces/
2 baking sheets

For the baking sheet:
baking parchment

For the yeast dough:
125 ml/4 fl oz (½ cup) milk
100 g/3½ oz (½ cup) butter
or margarine
500 g/18 oz plain (all-purpose)
flour
1 packet fast action dried yeast
50 g/1¾ oz (4 tablespoons)
sugar
3 drops vanilla essence
in 1 tablespoon sugar
2 medium eggs

For the filling:
80 g/3 oz (9 tablespoons)
custard powder
750 ml/1¼ pints (3½ cups) milk
80 g/2½ oz (⅜ cup) sugar
100 g/3½ oz raisins

For the apricot glaze:
3 tablespoons apricot preserve
4 teaspoons water

Per piece:
P: 5 g, F: 7 g, C: 35 g,
kJ: 925, kcal: 221

1 Warm the milk in a small pan and melt the butter or margarine in it.

2 To make the dough, carefully mix together the flour and dried yeast, then add the other ingredients and the warm margarine or butter mixture. Stir with a hand mixer with a kneading hook, first briefly at the lowest setting, then at the highest setting for about 5 minutes until it forms a smooth dough. Cover with a tea towel and put in a warm place until it has visibly increased in volume.

3 To make the custard filling, make a custard with custard powder, milk and sugar following the instructions on the packet but using only 750 ml/1¼ pints (3½ cups) milk. Leave to cool down, stirring occasionally. Stir the raisins into the filling. Line the baking sheet with baking parchment.

4 Preheat the oven. Dust the dough lightly with flour, remove from the bowl and knead again briefly on a lightly floured work surface. Roll out the dough into a rectangle (60 x 40 cm/24 x 16 in) and spread the custard on top. Roll up the dough starting from the short side, cut into slices about 2 cm/¾ in thick and put the slices on the baking sheet lined with baking parchment. Put the baking sheet with the slices in a warm place until they have visibly increased in volume. Put the baking sheet in the oven **for about 15 minutes**.

Top/bottom heat: about 200 °C/400 °F (preheated), Fan oven: about 180 °C/350 °F (preheated), Gas mark 6 (preheated).

5 To make the apricot glaze, rub the apricot jam through a sieve, add the water, boil to reduce and thicken a little while stirring. Brush the pastry with it immediately after removing from the oven. Put the custard snails on a rack to cool down.

Mohnstriezel

Preparation time:
about 60 minutes,
excluding rising time

Baking time:
about 60 minutes;

about 20 pieces

For the baking sheet:
some fat
baking parchment

For the yeast dough:
200 ml/7 fl oz (⅞ cup) water
150 g/5 oz (¾ cup) butter
or margarine
500 g/18 oz plain (all-purpose)
flour
1 packet fast action dried yeast
75 g/2½ oz (⅜ cup) sugar
3 drops vanilla essence
in 1 tablespoon sugar

For the filling:
300 g/10 oz poppy seeds
400 ml/14 fl oz (1¾ cups) milk
40 g/1½ oz (4½ tablespoons)
custard powder, vanilla flavour
100 ml/3½ fl oz (½ cup) milk
2 medium eggs
75 g/2½ oz (⅜ cup) sugar
75 g/2½ oz rusks

For the crumble:
100 g/3½ oz (1 cup) plain (all-purpose) flour
100 g/3½ oz blanched chopped
almonds
100 g/3½ oz (½ cup) sugar
100 g/3½ oz (½ cup) soft butter

For the coating:
3 tablespoons apricot preserve
2 teaspoons water
100 g/3½ oz icing
(confectioner's) sugar
1–2 tablespoons water

Per piece:
P: 9 g, F: 21 g, C: 47 g,
kJ: 1747, kcal: 417

1 Warm the water in a small pan and melt the butter or margarine in it. To make the dough, carefully mix together the flour and dried yeast, then add the other ingredients and the warm margarine or butter mixture. Stir with a hand mixer with a kneading hook, first briefly at the lowest setting, then at the highest setting for about 5 minutes until it forms a smooth dough. Cover with a tea towel and put in a warm place until it has visibly increased in volume.

2 To make the poppy seed filling, put the poppy seeds in the milk, bring to the boil and leave to swell for 10 minutes. Stir the milk into the custard powder and add to the poppy seed and milk mixture together with the eggs and sugar. Bring briefly to the boil again and allow to cool down. Put the rusks in a freezer bag, close it and hit them with a rolling pin to turn them into crumbs. Stir the rusk crumbs into the poppy seed mixture. Grease the baking sheet and line it with baking parchment.

3 Heat the oven top and bottom. Dust the dough lightly with flour, remove from the bowl and knead again briefly on a slightly floured work surface. Roll out into a rectangle (40 x 30 cm/16 x 12 in). Spread the poppy seed mixture on top, leaving 1 cm/⅜ in uncovered round the edges. Roll up the rectangle loosely starting with the longer side (photograph 1) and put on the baking sheet with the "seam" facing upward.

4 To make the crumble, sift the flour in a mixing bowl, add the almonds, sugar and softened butter and stir with a hand mixer with whisk until the crumble is the right texture. Brush a little water on the plaited bun, sprinkle the crumble on top and press down. Leave the plaited bun to rise again until it has increased visibly in volume. Put the baking sheet in the oven **for about 60 minutes**.

Top/bottom heat: about 180 °C/350 °F (preheated), Fan oven: about 160 °C/325 °F (not preheated), Gas mark 4 (not preheated).

continued on page 206 ⟹

5 To make the apricot glaze and the coating, bring the jam to the boil with a little water to reduce and thicken a little. Brush the plaited bun with it immediately after taking it out of the oven (photograph 3). Put on a rack to cool down. To make the coating, sift the icing sugar, add water and stir until thick and smooth. Brush the plaited bun with it.

Feiner Gugelhupf

Preparation time:
about 35 minutes,
excluding rising time

Baking time:
about 60 minutes;

about 16 pieces

For a gugelhupf mould
(diameter 24 cm/9½ in):
some fat

For the yeast dough:
200 ml/7 fl oz (⅞ cup) whipping cream
200 g/7 oz (1 cup) butter or margarine
500 g/18 oz plain (all-purpose) flour
1 packet fast action dried yeast
150 g/5 oz (¾ cup) sugar
3 drops vanilla essence in 1 tablespoon sugar
3 drops lemon essence
1 pinch salt
4 medium eggs
150 g/5 oz raisins
150 g/5 oz currants
100 g/3½ oz chopped blanched almonds

Per piece:
P: 7 g, F: 20 g, C: 47 g,
kJ: 1663, kcal: 397

1 Warm the whipping cream in a small pan and melt the butter or margarine in it.

2 To make the dough, carefully mix together the flour and dried yeast, add the other ingredients (except for the raisins, currants and almonds) and the warm margarine or butter mixture. Stir with a hand mixer with a kneading hook, first briefly at the lowest setting, then at the highest setting for about 5 minutes until it forms a smooth dough. Add the raisins, currants and almonds and stir briefly. Cover with a tea towel and put in a warm place until it has visibly increased in volume. Grease the gugelhupf mould.

3 Preheat the oven at the top and bottom. Knead the dough briefly with a hand mixer with kneading hook at the highest setting, transfer to the gugelhupf mould and put in a warm place until it has visibly increased in volume. Put the mould in the oven **for about 60 minutes**.

Top/bottom heat: about 180 °C/350 °F (preheated), Fan oven: about 160 °C/325 °F (not preheated), Gas mark 4 (not preheated).

4 Leave the cake in the mould for about 10 minutes after taking it out of the oven, then remove from the mould and put on a rack to cool down.

Streuselkuchen aus Thüringen (Thuringian crumb cake)

Preparation time:
about 35 minutes, excluding
rising and cooling time

Baking time:
about 20 minutes;

about 20 pieces

For a baking sheet
(40 x 30 cm / 16 x 12 in):
some fat

For the yeast dough:
200 ml / 7 fl oz (⅞ cup) milk
50 g / 2 oz (4 tablespoons) butter
or margarine
375 g / 13½ oz (3¾ cups) plain
(all-purpose) flour
1 packet fast action dried yeast
50 g / 1¾ oz (4 tablespoons)
sugar
3 drops vanilla essence
in 1 tablespoon sugar
1 medium egg

20 g / 1 oz (2 tablespoons) butter

For the crumble:
300 g / 10 oz (3 cups) plain (all-
purpose) flour
150 g / 5 oz (¾ cup) sugar
3 drops vanilla essence
in 1 tablespoon sugar
200 g / 7 oz (1 cup) soft butter
or margarine
10 g / ½ oz (¼ cup) cocoa powder

For pouring:
125 ml / 4 fl oz (½ cup) milk
60 g / 2½ oz (5 tablespoons)
butter

For finishing:
100 g / 3½ oz (½ cup) butter
icing (confectioner's) sugar

Per piece:
P: 5 g, F: 19 g, C: 38 g,
kJ: 1443, kcal: 345

1 Warm the milk in a small pan and melt the butter or margarine in it.

2 To make the dough, sift the flour into a mixing bowl and carefully stir in the dried yeast, then add the other ingredients and the warm margarine or butter mixture. Stir with a hand mixer with a kneading hook, first briefly at the lowest setting, then at the highest setting for about 5 minutes until it forms a smooth dough (photograph 1). Cover with a tea towel and put in a warm place until it has visibly increased in volume. Grease the baking sheet.

3 Preheat the oven. Dust the dough lightly with flour, remove from the mixing bowl and knead again briefly on a slightly floured work surface. Roll out the dough on a greased baking sheet. Melt the butter and brush the dough with it.

4 To make the crumble, stir the flour, sugar, vanilla sugar and softened butter or margarine in a mixing bowl. Stir with a hand mixer with whisk until the crumble has the right texture. Scatter half the crumble over the dough, leaving gaps. Add cocoa powder to the other half of the crumble, mix well and fill the gaps with it so as to create a dark and light pattern (photograph 2). Return the dough to a warm place until it has increased visibly in volume. Put the baking sheet in the oven **for about 20 minutes**.

Top/bottom heat: about 200 °C/400 °F (preheated), Fan oven: about 180 °C/350 °F (preheated), Gas mark 6 (preheated).

5 For pouring over the cake, heat the milk and melt the butter in it. With a spoon, distribute the melted butter mixture over the cake while it is still hot (photograph 3) and leave to cool on the baking sheet placed on a rack. When it is cool, melt the butter, brush it on the cake and dust icing sugar on top.

Butter cake

Preparation time:
about 20 minutes,
excluding rising time

Baking time:
about 15 minutes;

about 20 pieces

For a baking sheet
(40 x 30 cm / 16 x 12 in):
some fat

For the yeast dough:
200 ml/7 fl oz (⅞ cup) milk
50 g/2 oz (4 tablespoons) butter
375 g/13½ oz (3¾ cups) plain
(all-purpose) flour
1 packet fast action dried yeast
50 g/1¾ oz (4 table-spoons)
sugar
3 drops vanilla essence
in 1 tablespoon sugar
1 pinch salt
1 medium egg

For the topping:
100 g/3½ oz cold butter
75 g/2½ oz (⅜ cup) sugar
3 drops vanilla essence
in 1 tablespoon sugar
100 g/3½ oz blanched flaked
almonds

Per piece:
P: 4 g, F: 6 g, C: 21 g,
kJ: 632, kcal: 151

1 Warm the milk in a small pan and melt the butter in it.

2 To make the dough, carefully mix together the flour and dried yeast, then add the other ingredients and the warm butter mixture. Stir with a hand mixer with a kneading hook, first briefly at the lowest setting, then at the highest setting for about 5 minutes until it forms a smooth dough. Cover with a tea towel and put in a warm place until it has visibly increased in volume.

3 Meanwhile, preheat the oven and grease the baking sheet. Dust the dough lightly with flour, remove from the mixing bowl and knead again briefly on a lightly floured work surface. Roll out the dough on the baking sheet.

4 To make the topping, first make small depressions in the dough with the handle of a wooden spoon and scatter knobs of butter evenly over the dough (photograph 1). Mix together the sugar and vanilla sugar and sprinkle over the dough (photograph 2). Then sprinkle the almonds evenly on top (photograph 3). Put the dough in a warm place again until it has visibly increased in volume. Put the baking sheet in the oven **for about 15 minutes**.

Top/bottom heat: about 200 °C/400 °F (preheated), Fan oven: about 180 °C/350 °F (preheated), Gas mark 6 (preheated).

5 Put the baking sheet on a rack and leave the cake on it to cool.

Tip: Lightly whip 200 ml/7 fl oz (7/8 cup) cream and spread over the cake while it is still hot, immediately after taking it out of the oven.

Variation: To make butter cake with a nutty topping, coarsely chop 100 g/ 3½ oz hazelnuts or walnuts and sprinkle over the dough. Then scatter the knobs of butter and sprinkle the sugar on top. Dribble 8 tablespoons of whipping cream over the dough, put the dough in a warm place until it has visibly increased in volume and bake as described in the recipe.

Bienenstich

Preparation time:
about 50 minutes,
excluding rising time

Baking time:
about 15 minutes;

about 20 pieces

For a baking sheet
(40 x 30 cm / 16 x 12 in):
some fat

For the yeast dough:
200 ml / 7 fl oz (⅞ cup) milk
50 g / 2 oz (4 tablespoons) butter
or margarine
375 g / 13½ oz (3¾ cups) plain
(all-purpose) flour
1 packet fast action dried yeast
50 g / 1¾ oz (4 tablespoons)
sugar
3 drops vanilla essence
in 1 tablespoon sugar
1 pinch salt
1 medium egg

For the topping:
200 g / 7 oz (1 cup) butter
100 g / 3½ oz (½ cup) sugar
3 drops vanilla essence
in 1 tablespoon sugar
3 teaspoons honey
3 tablespoons whipping cream
200 g / 7 oz blanched chopped
almonds

For the filling:
80 g / 3 oz (9 tablespoons)
custard powder, vanilla flavour
750 ml / 1¼ pints (3½ cups) milk

100 g / 3½ oz (½ cup) sugar
100 g / 3½ oz (½ cup) butter

Per piece:
P: 6 g, F: 23 g, C: 33 g,
kJ: 1514, kcal: 361

1 Warm the milk in a small pan and melt the butter or margarine in it.

2 To make the dough, sift the plain flour in a mixing bowl, carefully mix with dried yeast, add the other ingredients and the warm margarine or butter mixture. Stir with a hand mixer with a kneading hook, first briefly at the lowest setting, then at the highest setting for about 5 minutes, until it forms smooth dough. Cover with a tea towel and put in a warm place until it has visibly increased in volume.

3 To make the topping, slowly heat the butter with the sugar, vanilla sugar, honey and cream while stirring, bring briefly to the boil and stir in the almonds. Leave the mixture to cool down, stirring occasionally. Grease the baking sheet.

4 Preheat the oven. Dust the dough lightly with flour, remove from the bowl and knead again briefly on a lightly floured work surface. Roll out and line the baking sheet with the dough. Spread the topping evenly on the dough (photograph 1) and put the baking sheet in a warm place again until the dough has visibly increased in volume. Put the baking sheet in the oven **for about 15 minutes**.

Top/bottom heat: about 200 °C/400 °F (preheated), Fan oven: about 180 °C/350 °F (preheated), Gas mark 6 (preheated).

5 Leave the cake on the baking sheet to cool down on a rack. Cut the cake in half vertically and then cut each half horizontally (photograph 2).

6 For the filling, make the custard with custard powder, milk and sugar following the instructions on the packet but, using only 750 ml/1¼ pints (3½ cups) milk, and stir the butter into the hot custard. Put the cream filling in the refrigerator, stirring occasionally. Spread the cold cream filling on the lower cake halves (photograph 3), then put the other halves on top.

Lüneburger Buchweizentorte

(Lüneburger buckwheat fancy cake)

Preparation time:
about 55 minutes,
excluding cooling time

Baking time:
about 30 minutes;

about 16 pieces

For a springform tin
(diameter 26 cm/10 in):
some fat
baking parchment

For the sponge mixture:
5 medium eggs
4 teaspoons hot water
150 g/5 oz (¾ cup) sugar
3 drops vanilla essence
in 1 tablespoon sugar
1–2 drops almond essence
150 g/5 oz buckwheat flour
1 level teaspoon baking powder
100 g/3½ oz ground hazelnut
kernels

For the filling:
1 packet powdered gelatine
2 tablespoons cold water
600 ml/21 oz (2½ cups) chilled
whipping cream
2–3 drops natural vanilla essence
in 1–2 tablespoons sugar
2 jars (each 395 g/14 oz) wild
cranberries

For the topping:
ground pistachio nuts

Per piece:
P: 5 g, F: 17 g, C: 24 g,
kJ: 1142, kcal: 272

1 Preheat the oven, grease the bottom of the springform tin and line with baking parchment.

2 To make the sponge, whisk the eggs with the hot water in a mixing bowl using a hand mixer with whisk at the highest setting for 1 minute until foamy. Mix together the sugar and vanilla sugar, sprinkle into the egg mixture over a period of 1 minute while stirring, and continue whisking for another 2 minutes. Stir in the almond essence. Mix together the buckwheat flour and baking powder, and stir quickly into the mixture at the lowest setting. Stir in the hazelnuts in the same way. Spoon the sponge into the springform tin, smooth out the surface and put in the oven **for about 30 minutes**.

Top/bottom heat: about 180 °C/350 °F (preheated), Fan oven: about 160 °C/325 °F (preheated), Gas mark 4 (preheated).

3 Remove the cake from the springform tin and turn out onto a wire rack lined with baking parchment. Then peel off the baking parchment on which it was baked and cut the cake twice horizontally. Put the bottom layer on a cake plate.

4 To make the filling, stir the gelatine in the water in a small pan, leave to soak for 10 minutes and then warm up while stirring until it is dissolved. Beat together the whipping cream and vanilla sugar until almost stiff, add the lukewarm gelatine mixture and continue whisking until the cream mixture is very stiff.

5 Spread one jar of cranberries on the bottom layer, leaving 1 cm/⅜ in uncovered around the edge. Cover with about 3 tablespoons cream and put the middle layer on top. Spread the other jar of cranberries on top and cover with the cream. Finally, put the top layer in place. Coat the top and sides of the torte with cream and decorate the sides with a wavy pattern using a cake comb. Put the rest of the cream in a piping bag with a small nozzle, decorate the cake and refrigerate until serving. Garnish the cake with the rest of the cranberries and pistachio nuts just before serving.

Tip: The cake tastes best when made the day before and refrigerated until it is served.

Schwarzwälder Kirschtorte

(Black Forest cherry gâteau)

Preparation time:
about 60 minutes,
excluding cooling time

Baking time:
about 45 minutes;

about 16 pieces

For a springform tin
(diameter 28 cm/11 in):
some fat
baking parchment

For the dough:
125 g/4½ oz (⅝ cup) plain (all-purpose) flour
10 g/⅓ oz (1 tablespoon) cocoa powder
1 pinch baking powder
50 g/2 oz (¼ cup) sugar
3 drops vanilla essence
in 1 tablespoon sugar
2 teaspoons Kirsch
75 g/3 oz (5 tablespoons) soft butter or margarine

For the sponge mixture:
4 medium eggs
100 g/3½ oz (½ cup) sugar
3 drops vanilla essence
in 1 tablespoon sugar
100 g/3½ oz (1 cup) plain (all-purpose) flour
½ level teaspoon baking powder
25 g/1 oz (3 tablespoons) cornflour (cornstarch)
10 g/⅓ oz (1 tablespoon) cocoa powder
generous pinch powdered cinnamon

For the filling:
1 can sour cherries, drained weight 350 g/12 oz
or 500 g/18 oz sour cherries
75 g/2½ oz (⅜ cup) sugar

1 Preheat the oven and grease the bottom of the springform tin.

2 To make the dough, carefully mix together the flour, cocoa powder and baking powder and sift into a mixing bowl. Add the other ingredients for the dough and stir with a hand-mixer with a kneading hook, first briefly at the lowest setting, then at the highest setting for about 5 minutes, to make a smooth dough. Then form into a ball using your hands. Roll out and line the greased bottom of the springform tin, prick several times with a fork and put the ring round the base again. Put the springform tin on a shelf into the oven **for about 15 minutes.**

Top/bottom heat: about 180° C/350° F (preheated), Fan oven: about 160° C/325° F (preheated), Gas mark 4 (preheated).

3 Turn the base out immediately after removing from the oven and leave on a wire rack to cool down. Now clean the springform tin, grease the base and line with baking parchment.

4 To make the sponge mixture, whisk the eggs in a mixing bowl using a hand mixer with whisk at the highest setting for 1 minute until foamy. Mix together the sugar and vanilla sugar, sprinkle slowly into the egg mixture for a period of 1 minute while stirring and continue whisking for another 2 minutes. Mix together the flour, baking powder, cornstarch, cocoa powder and cinnamon, sift and stir quickly into the mixture at the lowest setting. Spoon the sponge mixture in the mould, smooth the surface flat and put on a shelf in the oven. **Bake for about 30 minutes at the same temperature as the dough.**

5 Loosen the ring and remove. Turn the sponge out onto a wire rack lined with baking parchment and leave to cool down. Then carefully peel off the baking parchment on which it was baked. Cut the sponge in half horizontally.

6 To make the filling, drain the cherries thoroughly in a colander, save the juice and reserve 250 ml/8 fl oz (1 cup). Alternatively wash fresh sour cherries, remove the stalks and stones, stir in the sugar and leave to draw out the juice for a few minutes. Put the cherries in a pan and bring to the boil. Then drain in a colander, reserve the juice and leave to cool down. Measure 250 ml/8 fl oz (1 cup) of this juice, and if necessary top up with water. Put 12 cherries for garnishing the cake to one side draining them on kitchen paper.

7 Make the glaze with juice, arrowroot and sugar. Take 250 ml/8 fl oz (1 cup) cherry juice. Blend 2 teaspoons arrowroot with a little of the liquid, then stir in the rest of the liquid. Bring to the boil and simmer for ½–1 minute until it is clear, stirring occasionally. Stir in the cherries and leave the mixture to cool down, then add the Kirsch. Stir the gelatine into water in a small pan, leave to soak for 10 minutes, then warm up while stirring until the gelatine has dissolved. Whip the cream until nearly stiff, whisk in the lukewarm gelatine mixture and continue whipping until very stiff. Sift the icing (confectioner's) sugar, mix together with the vanilla sugar and stir into the cream mixture.

8 Put the dough base on a cake plate and spread the cherry mixture on top, leaving 1 cm/⅜ in uncovered round the edge. Spread one-third of the cream mixture on top (photograph 1, page 216). Next put the lower sponge layer on top, press down lightly and spread half of the remaining cream on top of it. Put the second sponge layer on top and press down lightly again. Put 3 tablespoons of the whipped cream mixture in a piping bag with a star-shaped nozzle and put to one side. Cover the top and sides of the cake evenly with the rest of the cream mixture. Now decorate the top of the cake with the whipped cream in the piping bag (photograph 2, page 216) and grated chocolate or chocolate shavings. Garnish with the cherries you have put aside. Refrigerate for at least 2 hours.

Tip: Soak the sponge layers with 3 tablespoons of Kirsch.

For the glaze:
2 teaspoons arrowroot
4 teaspoons sugar
250 ml/8 fl oz (1 cup) cherry juice, from the can
about 2 tablespoons Kirsch
1 sachet powdered gelatine, white
3 tablespoons cold water

800 ml/28 fl oz (3½ cups) cooled whipping cream
40 g/1½ oz (⅜ cup) icing (confectioner's) sugar
3 drops vanilla essence in 1 tablespoon sugar

Per piece:
P: 6 g, F: 21 g, C: 35 g, kJ: 1490, kcal: 356

Almond and cherry cake

Preparation time:
about 25 minutes

Baking time:
about 45 minutes;

about 20 pieces

For a baking sheet with sides
about 2 cm/¾ in high
(40 x 30 cm/16 x 12 in)
or a roasting tin:
some fat
breadcrumbs

For the filling:
2 jars sour cherries (drained
weight 350 g/12 oz each)

For the sponge mixture:
whites of 9 medium eggs
yolks of 9 medium eggs
250 g/9 oz (1⅛ cup) sugar
3 drops vanilla essence
in 1 tablespoon sugar
1–2 drops almond essence
1 pinch ground cinnamon
2 teaspoons Kirsch
300 g/10 oz unblanched,
ground almonds
100 g/3½ oz breadcrumbs

Per piece:
P: 7 g, F: 11 g, C: 24 g,
kJ: 959, kcal: 229

1 Preheat the oven, grease the bottom of the baking sheet or roasting tin and sprinkle with breadcrumbs. Drain the cherries thoroughly in a sieve.

2 To make the sponge mixture, put the egg whites in a mixing bowl and whisk until very stiff and put to one side. Mix together the egg yolks with the sugar, vanilla sugar, almond essence, cinnamon and Kirsch in a large mixing bowl with a hand mixer with whisk at the highest setting until foamy. Fold in the almonds and breadcrumbs, then also fold in the stiff egg whites.

3 Spread the cake mixture on the baking sheet. Arrange the cherries on the cake mixture. Put the baking sheet in the oven **for about 45 minutes.**

Top/bottom heat: about 180 °C/350 °F (preheated), Fan oven: about 160 °C/325 °F (preheated), Gas mark 4 (preheated).

4 Put the baking sheet or roasting tin on a rack and leave the sponge to cool down.

Tips: Dust the almond and cherry cake with icing (confectioner's) sugar before serving.
This cake freezes very well. First let it cool down completely, then put it on a paper base in a freezer bag or freezer box.
To beat the egg whites very stiff, the bowl and whisk must be absolutely fat free and the egg white must not contain a trace of egg yolk.

Mandarin orange and cheese slices

Preparation time:
about 45 minutes,
excluding cooling time

Baking time:
about 10 minutes;

about 10 pieces

For a baking sheet
(40 x 30 cm/16 x 12 in):
some fat
baking parchment

For the sponge mixture:
3 medium eggs
2 tablespoons hot water
150 g/5 oz (¾ cup) sugar
3 drops vanilla essence
in 1 tablespoon sugar
100 g/3½ oz (1 cup) plain (all-purpose) flour
1 level teaspoon baking powder
50 g/2 oz (6 tablespoons) cornflour (cornstarch)

For the filling:
2 cans mandarin oranges
(drained weight 175 g/6 oz each)
100 ml/3½ fl oz (½ cup) mandarin juice (from the cans)
6 sheets gelatine, white
500 g/18 oz curd cheese (low fat)
150 g/5 oz (¾ cup) sugar
3 drops vanilla essence
in 1 tablespoon sugar
grated zest of 1 untreated lemon
4 teaspoons lemon juice
200 ml/7 fl oz (⅞ cup) chilled whipping cream

Per piece:
P: 12 g, F: 8 g, C: 54 g,
kJ: 1445, kcal: 345

1 Preheat the oven, grease the baking sheet and line with baking parchment. Fold the baking parchment to make a rim along the open side of the baking sheet.

2 To make the sponge mixture, whisk the eggs with the hot water in a mixing bowl using a hand mixer with whisk at the highest setting for 1 minute until foamy. Mix together the sugar and vanilla sugar, sprinkle into the egg mixture over a period of 1 minute while stirring, and continue whisking for another 2 minutes. Mix together the flour, baking powder and cornstarch, sift and stir quickly into the mixture at the lowest setting. Spread the sponge mixture on the baking sheet and put in the oven **for about 10 minutes**.

Top/bottom heat: about 200 °C/400 °F (preheated), Fan oven: about 180 °C/350 °F (preheated), Gas mark 6 (preheated).

3 Carefully loosen the sponge along the edges and turn onto baking parchment, sprinkled with sugar. Brush the baking parchment on which the sponge was baked with a little water and peel off gently. Leave the sponge to cool down and then cut in two vertically to make 2 rectangles (30 x 20 cm/12 x 8 in).

4 To make the filling, drain the mandarins in a sieve, reserving 100 ml/ 3½ fl oz (½ cup) of the juice. Soak the gelatine following the instructions on the packet. Stir together the curd cheese, sugar, vanilla sugar, lemon zest and lemon juice. Heat the mandarin juice. Squeeze out the gelatine, add to the mandarin juice and stir until dissolved. Stir 4 tablespoons of the curd cheese mixture in the dissolved gelatine using a whisk, then stir in the rest of the curd cheese mixture.

5 Whip the cream until stiff. When the curd cheese mixture begins to thicken, fold in the cream with the mandarins. Spread the filling on one of the rectangles, put the other rectangle on top (with the underside facing upward) and press down lightly. Smooth the sides flat and refrigerate for about 2 hours.

Tip: Dust with icing sugar before serving and cut into portions.

Rolled slices (Coffee slices)

Preparation time:
about 40 minutes

Baking time:
about 25 minutes;

about 10 pieces

For the baking sheet:
some fat
baking parchment

For the cake mixture:
150 g/5 oz (1⅓ cup) plain (all-purpose) flour
4 level teaspoons baking powder
50 g/1½ oz (4 tablespoons) sugar
1 teaspoon vanilla essence
1 pinch salt
75 g/3 oz curd cheese (low fat)
50 ml /1½ fl oz (3 tablespoons) milk
50 ml /1½ fl oz (3 tablespoons) cooking oil, e.g. sunflower oil

For the filling:
100 g/3½ oz marzipan
50 g/2 oz (4 tablespoons) soft butter
1 medium egg
25 g/1 oz candied lemon peel
125 g/5 oz raisins
50 g/2 oz chopped hazelnut kernels
1 pinch ground cinnamon
½ teaspoon rum essence

For the icing:
80 g/3 oz (⅝ cup) icing (confectioner's) sugar
2–4 teaspoons rum

Per piece:
P: 6 g, F: 17 g, C: 39 g,
kJ: 1411, kcal: 337

1 Preheat the oven. Grease the baking sheet with fat and line it baking parchment.

2 To make the dough, carefully mix together the flour and baking powder and sift into the mixing bowl. Add the other ingredients and stir with a hand mixer with kneading hook, first briefly at the lowest setting, then at the highest setting, to make a smooth dough. Do not knead too long or the dough may become sticky. Then shape into a cylinder on a floured work surface.

3 For the filling, cut the marzipan into small pieces, add the softened butter and egg and stir with a hand mixer until the mixture is smooth and homogenous. Finely chop the candied lemon peel and add to the mixture together with the raisins, hazelnuts, cinnamon and rum essence.

4 Roll out the dough on a lightly floured work surface to form a square (30 x 30 cm/12 x 12 in) and cover with the marzipan mixture. Sprinkle the raisin mixture on top (photograph 1) and press down lightly. Roll up the dough and put on the prepared baking sheet. Make a cut 2.5 cm/ 1 in deep along almost the whole length of the cake, about 25 cm/ 10 in, but without cutting through to the ends (photograph 2), pull slightly apart and press to flatten. Put the baking sheet in the oven **for about 25 minutes**.

Top/bottom heat: about 180 °C/350 °F (preheated), Fan oven: about 160 °C/325 °F (preheated), Gas mark 4 (preheated).

5 For the icing, sift the icing sugar and stir enough rum to make a thick glaze. Spread this over the cake immediately after removing it from the oven using a pastry brush (photograph 3). Leave to cool and cut into thin strips.

Cheese and apple with crumble

Preparation time:
about 45 minutes

Baking time:
about 60 minutes;
about 20 pieces

For a baking sheet
(40 x 30 cm / 16 x 12 in):
some fat
aluminium foil

For the cake mixture:
300 g/10 oz (3 cups) plain (all-purpose) flour
3 level teaspoons baking powder
75 g/2½ oz (⅜ cup) sugar
3 drops vanilla essence
in 1 tablespoon sugar
1 pinch salt
150 g/5 oz curd cheese (low fat)
100 ml/3½ fl oz (½ cup) milk
100 ml/3½ fl oz (½ cup) cooking oil

For the filling:
1.5 kg/3¼ lb sharp apples
whites of 4 medium eggs
150 g/5 oz (¾ cup) soft butter or margarine
100 g/3½ oz (½ cup) sugar
2–3 drops lemon essence
yolks of 4 medium eggs
850 g/30 oz curd cheese (low fat)
50 g/2 oz (¼ cup) semolina flour

For the crumble:
200 g/7 oz (2 cups) plain (all-purpose) flour
70 g/3 oz blanched ground almonds
150 g/5 oz (¾ cup) sugar
½ teaspoon ground cinnamon
150 g/5 oz (¾ cup) soft butter or margarine

Per piece:
P: 12 g, F: 22 g, C: 47 g,
kJ: 1804, kcal: 431

1 Preheat the oven at the top and bottom and grease the baking sheet with fat.

2 To make the dough, mix together the flour and baking powder, sift into a mixing bowl and add the other ingredients. Stir with a hand mixer with kneading hook, first briefly at the lowest setting, then at the highest setting until the dough is formed. Do not knead too long or the dough may become sticky. Then shape into a roll on a floured work surface. Roll out the dough and place a strip of aluminium foil along the open end of the baking sheet to form an edge.

3 To make the topping, wash, peel, quarter and core the apples and cut them into thin segments. Arrange the segments overlapping on the base. Whisk the egg whites until they are very stiff with a hand mixer with whisk and put to one side. Put the softened butter or margarine in a mixing bowl and whisk with a hand mixer with whisk until smooth and homogenous. Add the sugar, lemon essence, egg yolk, curd cheese and semolina flour and whisk to incorporate all the ingredients. Fold the beaten egg whites into the curd cheese mixture. Cover the apples with this mixture.

4 To make the crumble, sift the flour and add the almonds, sugar, cinnamon and softened butter or margarine. Stir together with a hand mixer with whisk until the crumble has the right texture. Sprinkle the crumble over the curd cheese mixture and put the baking sheet in the oven **for about 60 minutes**.

Top/bottom heat: about 180 °C/350 °F (preheated), Fan oven: about 160 °C/325 °F (not preheated), Gas mark 4 (not preheated).

5 Put the baking sheet on a rack and leave the cake to cool down it.

Tip: Instead of the crumble, you can sprinkle 50 g/2 oz peeled, flaked almonds and 50 g/2 oz raisins over the curd cheese mixture.

Cheese strudel

Preparation time:
about 40 minutes,
excluding resting time

Baking time:
about 45 minutes;

about 12 pieces

For the baking sheet:
baking parchment

For the strudel:
125 g/4½ oz (1¼ cups) plain
(all-purpose) flour
1 pinch salt, 1 medium egg
4 teaspoons lukewarm water
3–4 teaspoons cooking oil

For the filling:
40 g/1½ oz (3 tablespoons) soft
margarine or butter
40 g/1½ oz (4 tablespoons)
sugar
1 medium egg
2 teaspoons lemon juice
250 g/9 oz curd cheese (low fat)
4 teaspoons vanilla flavoured
custard powder
4 teaspoons whipping cream
1 cans apricot halves (drained
weight 240 g/8½ oz)

For the coating and topping:
40 g/1½ oz (3 tablespoons)
butter
50 g/2 oz raisins

For dusting:
some icing (confectioner's) sugar

Per piece:
P: 5 g, F: 9 g, C: 19 g,
kJ: 747, kcal: 178

1 To make the dough, mix together the flour and baking powder, sift into a mixing bowl and add the other ingredients. Stir with a hand mixer with kneading hook, first briefly at the lowest setting, then at the highest setting until a smooth dough is formed. Boil some water in a small pan, pour out the water and wipe dry. Put the dough in the hot pan lined with baking parchment, cover with the lid and let stand for 30 minutes. Meanwhile, line the baking sheet with baking parchment and preheat the oven top and bottom.

2 For the filling, stir the softened margarine or butter until smooth and supple. Stir in the sugar, egg, lemon juice, curd cheese, custard powder and cream. Drain the apricot halves thoroughly in a sieve and cut into small pieces. Cut the dough in half and roll out on a floured tea towel to make rectangle measuring 40 x 30 cm/16 x 12 in.

3 Melt the butter. Brush the dough halves with some of this melted butter. Spread half the filling over two-thirds of each dough half, leaving about 3 cm/1¼ in uncovered along the edges, and sprinkle half the raisins and apricot pieces on top. Fold the uncovered part along the long sides onto the filling. Using the tea towel to help the process, roll up the dough halves starting from the short side and press the ends together. Put the strudel on the baking sheet, brush with a little butter and put in the oven **for about 45 minutes**.

Top/bottom heat: about 180 °C/350 °F (preheated), Fan oven: about 160 °C/325 °F (not preheated), Gas mark 4 (not preheated).

4 After 30 minutes in the oven, brush the strudel with the rest of the melted butter. After removing from the oven, put the strudel (without taking it off the baking sheet) on a rack to cool down. Alternatively, serve it hot and dust with icing (confectioner's) sugar if desired.

Tip: The strudel may also be served with hot vanilla sauce. When crisping up defrosted strudel, brush with melted butter and bake for 10 minutes at the temperature recommended in the recipe.

Apfelstrudel (Apple strudel)

Preparation time:
about 50 minutes,
excluding resting time

Baking time:
about 50 minutes;

about 12 pieces

For the baking sheet:
some fat

For the strudel dough:
200 g/7 oz (2 cups) plain (all-purpose) flour
1 pinch salt
75 ml/3 fl oz lukewarm water
50 g/2 oz (4 tablespoons) melted margarine or butter or 4 tablespoons cooking oil

For the filling:
1– 1.5 kg/2¼–3¼ lb apples, such as Cox Orange, Elstar
2–3 drops rum essence
1–2 drops lemon essence
75 g/2½ oz (⅜ cup) margarine or butter
50 g/2 oz breadcrumbs
50 g/2 oz raisins
100 g/3½ oz (½ cup) sugar
3 drops vanilla essence in 1 tablespoon sugar
50 g/2 oz chopped blanched almonds

Per piece:
P: 2 g, F: 11 g, C: 37 g,
kJ: 1096, kcal: 262

1 To make the dough, sift the flour into a mixing bowl, add the other ingredients for the dough and stir with a hand mixer with a kneading hook, first briefly at the lowest setting, then at the highest setting, to make a smooth dough. Boil some water in a small pan, pour out the water and wipe dry. Put the dough in the hot pan lined with baking parchment, cover with the lid and let stand for 30 minutes. Meanwhile, grease the baking sheet and preheat the oven at the top and bottom.

2 For the filling, wash, peel, quarter, core and cut the apples into small pieces. Stir in the rum and lemon essence. Melt the margarine or butter. Roll out the dough on a large floured tea towel, brush lightly with a little melted butter or margarine, then stretch using your hands to make a rectangle (of 70 x 50 cm/27½ in x 20 in). Trim the edges if they are thicker than the rest of the rectangle. Brush the dough with two-thirds of the melted butter or margarine and sprinkle the breadcrumbs on top, leaving about 3 cm/1¼ in uncovered.

3 Sprinkle the apple pieces, raisins, sugar, vanilla sugar and almonds on top. Fold the edges of the short sides that have been left uncovered over the filling. Using the cloth to help you, roll the dough, starting from the longer side, and press the ends together tightly. Put the strudel on the prepared baking sheet, brush with a little fat and put the baking sheet in the oven **for about 50 minutes**.

Top/bottom heat: about 180 °C/350 °F (preheated), Fan oven: about 160 °C/325 °F (not preheated), Gas mark 4 (not preheated).

4 After 30 minutes baking time, brush the strudel with the rest of the melted butter or margarine. After removing the strudel from the oven leave it cool down on the baking sheet placed on a rack. The strudel can be served hot or cold.

Tips: This can be served with vanilla sauce, flavoured with cinnamon. You could also make 2 small strudels instead of 1 large one.

Schillerlocken (Cream horns)

Preparation time:
about 30 minutes, excluding
defrosting and cooling time

Baking time:
about 15 minutes
per baking sheet;

12 pieces/2 baking sheets

For the baking sheet:
some fat
some water
6 cream horn moulds

For the pastry:
1 packet (450 g/16 oz) frozen
puff pastry or 1 basic recipe puff
pastry

In addition:
yolk of 1 medium egg
2 teaspoons milk
50 g/2 oz blanched flaked
almonds
60 g/2 oz (¼ cup) sugar crystals

For the filling:
400 ml/14 fl oz (1¾ cups) chilled
whipping cream
2 heaped teaspoons sugar
2 teaspoons each orange
marmalade, raspberry jam,
grated chocolate

Per piece:
P: 4 g, F: 22 g, C: 22 g,
kJ: 1254, kcal: 300

1 Defrost the puff pastry following the instructions on the packet or make it yourself following the instructions in the basic recipe. Preheat the oven. Grease the baking sheet and sprinkle with a little water.

2 Put half the dough layers on top of each other (or using half the dough) on a floured work surface and roll into a rectangle (40 x 24 cm/16 x 9½ in). Using a pastry wheel, cut the dough lengthways into 6 strips 4 cm/1½ in wide.

3 Rinse 6 cream horn moulds in cold water. Starting from the pointed end, wrap each strip round the metal mould in such a way that it always overlaps slightly (photograph 1).

4 Beat together the egg yolk and milk and brush the cream horns with it. Mix together the almonds and sugar crystals and roll the horns in this mixture (photograph 2). Put the horn moulds on the prepared baking sheet and put the baking sheet in the oven **for about 15 minutes**.

Top/bottom heat: about 200 °C/400 °F (preheated), Fan oven: about 180 °C/350 °F (preheated), Gas mark 6 (preheated).

5 Remove the cream horns immediately from the baking sheet and put on a rack to cool down. Make the next batch of 6 cream horns with the rest of the dough in the same way and bake.

6 To make the filling, whip the cream stiff with sugar. Mix the orange marmalade, raspberry jam and grated chocolate each with one-third of the cream. Pipe the filling into the cream horns using a piping bag with a star-shaped nozzle (photograph 3). Then serve the cream horns.

Crispy cushion pastries

Preparation time:
about 40 minutes, excluding
defrosting and cooling time

Baking time:
about 20 minutes;

about 8 pieces

For the baking sheet:
some fat
some water

For the pastry:
½ packet (225 g/8 oz) frozen
puff pastry or ½ basic recipe puff
pastry

For coating:
1 egg yolk
2 teaspoons milk

For the crumble:
175 g/7 oz (2 cups) plain (all-
purpose) flour
75 g/2½ oz (⅜ cup) sugar
100 g/3½ oz (½ cup) soft butter

For the filling:
250 ml/8 fl oz (1 cup) chilled
whipping cream
25 g/1 oz (¼ cup) icing
(confectioner's) sugar
150 g/5 oz ready-made custard,
vanilla flavoured (from the cool
cabinet)

For dusting:
some icing (confectioner's) sugar

Per piece:
P: 6 g, F: 30 g, C: 48 g,
kJ: 2034, kcal: 486

1 Defrost the puff pastry following the instructions on the packet or make it yourself following the instructions in the basic recipe but halving the amounts. Preheat the oven. Grease the baking sheet and sprinkle with a little water.

2 Put the dough layers on top of each other (or using half the dough) on a floured work surface and roll into a rectangle (40 x 20 cm/16 x 8 in). Using a sharp knife, cut 8 squares (10 x 10 cm/4 x 4 in) and put on the prepared baking sheet. Stir together the egg yolk and milk and brush over the squares.

3 To make the crumble, sift the flour into a mixing bowl, add the sugar and softened butter and stir with a hand mixer with whisk until the crumble has the right texture. Sprinkle the crumble evenly over the squares and put the baking sheet in the oven **for about 20 minutes**.

Top/bottom heat: about 200 °C/400 °F (preheated), Fan oven: about 180 °C/350 °F (preheated), Gas mark 6 (preheated).

4 Put the cushion pastries on a rack to cool down and carefully cut off the top of each square with a serrated knife.

5 To make the filling, whip the cream stiff with the sifted icing sugar and fold into the custard. Spread the custard cream on the base of the squares with a piping bag or tablespoon, put the top back on and dust with icing sugar.

Doughnuts (Berliner)

Preparation and baking time:
about 60 minutes,
excluding rising time;

16 pieces

For the yeast dough:
125 ml/4 fl oz (½ cup) milk
100 g/3½ oz (½ cup) butter
or margarine
500 g/18 oz plain (all-purpose)
flour
1 packet fast action dried yeast
30 g/1 oz (3 tablespoons) sugar
3 drops vanilla essence
in 1 tablespoon sugar
1–2 drops almond essence
1 level teaspoon salt
2 medium eggs
yolk of 1 medium egg

For frying:
frying oil

For coating:
some sugar

For the filling:
300 g/10 oz jam to taste
or 250 g/9 oz plum purée or
jelly

Per piece:
P: 5 g, F: 13 g, C: 25 g,
kJ: 1001, kcal: 239

1 Warm the milk in a small pan and melt the butter or margarine in it.

2 For the dough, sift the flour into a mixing bowl, add the dried yeast and mix well. Then add the other ingredients and the warm milk-fat mixture. Stir briefly with a hand mixer with a whisk at the lowest setting, then at the highest setting for about 5 minutes to make a smooth dough. Cover the dough and put in a warm place to rise until it has visibly increased in volume.

3 Meanwhile, heat the oil in a large saucepan or deep-fryer to a temperature of about 180 °C/350 °F so that bubbles form round a wooden spoon handle lowered into it.

4 Sprinkle the dough lightly with flour, take it out of the bowl and knead briefly again on the work surface. Divide the dough into 16 pieces of similar size. Roll each piece into a ball on the work surface, using your thumbs and the palms of your hands. Make sure that there are no tears in the dough. Place the dough balls between 2 floured tea towels and leave until they are visibly increased in volume.

5 Put the dough balls a few at a time in the hot oil and fry until golden brown all over. Remove from the oil with a skimming ladle and drain on kitchen paper. Coat the doughnuts in sugar when still hot and put on a rack to cool down. For the filling, rub the jam through a sieve or stir the jelly or plum purée until smooth and put in a piping bag with a small nozzle. Pipe the filling into each doughnut along the pale ring round the ball.

Tip: The doughnuts can also be glazed with icing (confectioner's) sugar. To do this, sift the icing sugar and stir just enough water into it to make a spreadable glaze.

Eberswald fritters (Spritzkuchen)

Preparation and baking time:
about 90 minutes;

about 25 pieces

For frying:
frying oil
baking parchment
some fat

For the choux pastry:
250 ml/8 fl oz (1 cup) water
50 g/2 oz (4 tablespoons) butter
or margarine
150 g/5 oz (1⅓ cup) plain (all-
purpose) flour
30 g/1 oz (3 tablespoons)
cornflour (cornstarch)
25 g/1 oz (2 tablespoons) sugar
3 drops vanilla essence
in 1 tablespoon sugar
5–6 medium eggs
1 level teaspoon baking powder

For the icing:
300 g/10 oz (2 cups) icing
(confectioner's) sugar
about 2 tablespoons lemon juice
hot water

Per piece:
P: 2 g, F: 6 g, C: 19 g,
kJ: 592, kcal: 141

1 Heat the oil in a large saucepan or deep-fryer to a temperature of about 180 °C/350 °F so that bubbles form round the wooden spoon handle lowered into it. Cut the baking parchment into squares (about 10 x 10 cm/4 x 4 in) and grease.

2 For the dough, bring the water to the boil together with the butter or margarine. Remove the pan from the heat. Mix together the flour and cornflour, sift and add all at once to the hot liquid. Stir into a smooth lump of dough, then continue cooking for 1 minute stirring continuously (photograph 1) and transfer to a mixing bowl.

3 Incorporate the sugar and vanilla sugar into the dough with a hand mixer with kneading hook at the highest setting. Beat the last egg and add just enough to the dough to make it shiny, and also so that it hangs from the spoon without dropping off. Only add the baking powder when the dough is cold.

4 Put the dough, in small amounts, in a piping bag with a large star-shaped nozzle and pipe onto the squares of baking parchment in the shape of small wreaths (photograph 2). Loosen the wreaths by dipping the baking parchment square into the fat and fry until golden brown on both sides (photograph 3). Remove the fritters from the oil with a skimming ladle, drain on kitchen paper and put on a rack to cool down.

5 For the icing, sift the icing sugar, stir in enough lemon juice to make a thick mixture and coat the fritters with it.

Cinnamon stars

Preparation time:
about 60 minutes

Baking time:
about 25 minutes
per baking sheet;

about 40 pieces/
2 baking sheets

For the baking sheet:
baking parchment

For the pastry:
whites of 3 medium eggs
250 g/9 oz (1¾ cups) icing
(confectioner's) sugar
3 drops vanilla essence
in 1 tablespoon sugar
1–2 drops almond essence
1 level teaspoon ground
cinnamon
about 400 g/14 oz unblanched
ground almonds or hazelnut
kernels

In addition:
some icing (confectioner's) sugar

Per piece:
P: 2 g, F: 5 g, C: 7 g,
kJ: 354, kcal: 85

1 Preheat the oven and line the baking sheet with baking parchment.

2 For the dough, whisk the egg whites with a hand mixer with whisk at the highest setting until they form stiff peaks. Sift the icing sugar and stir in little by little. Reserve 2 well-heaped tablespoons of whisked egg white to spread on the stars.

3 Add the vanilla sugar, almond essence, cinnamon and 150 g/5 oz of the almonds or hazelnuts to the whisked egg white and stir carefully with the hand mixer at the lowest setting. Using your hands, incorporate enough of the rest of the almonds or hazelnuts into the mixture so that the dough hardly sticks.

4 Roll out the dough on a work-surface dusted with icing sugar to a thickness of a good 5 mm/3/16 in. Cut out the star shapes, put on the prepared baking sheet and cover with the reserved whisked egg white. The egg white must be soft enough to be spread flat on the dough; if necessary, add a few drops of water. Put the baking sheet in the oven **for about 25 minutes**.

Top/bottom heat: about 140 °C/275 °F (preheated), Fan oven: about 120 °C/250 °F (preheated), Gas mark 1 (preheated).

5 The biscuits should still feel a little soft underneath when you take them out of the oven. Slide the baking parchment with the stars on top off the baking sheet and put on a rack to cool down.

Tip: It is easier to cut out the stars if the cutter is dipped regularly in water while using it.
The stars will remain moist if they are stored in a well-sealed container.
To whisk the egg whites, the bowl and whisk must be completely free of fat, and the egg white must contain no trace of egg yolk.

Vanilla crescents

1 Preheat the oven and line with baking parchment.

2 For the dough, mix together the flour and baking powder and sift into a mixing bowl. Add the rest of the ingredients for the dough and stir with a hand mixer with kneading hook, first briefly at the lowest setting, then at the highest setting to make a smooth dough. Then shape into a ball with your hands.

3 Roll out the dough into cylinders the thickness of a pencil and cut into pieces 5–6 cm/2–2½ in long (photograph 1), then roll out the ends a little thinner (photograph 2). Place the crescents on the prepared baking sheet and put the baking sheet in the oven **for about 60 minutes**.

Top/bottom heat: about 180 °C/350 °F (preheated), Fan oven: about 160 °C/325 °F (preheated), Gas mark 4 (preheated).

4 Remove the crescents from the baking sheet with the baking parchment and put on a rack to cool down. Sift the icing (confectioner's) sugar, stir in the vanilla sugar and sprinkle on the crescents while they are hot (photograph 3). Leave to cool down.

Preparation time:
about 60 minutes

Baking time:
about 10 minutes
per baking sheet;

about 90 pieces/
3 baking sheets

For the baking sheet:
baking parchment

For the shortcrust pastry:
250 g/9 oz (2½ cups) plain (all-purpose) flour
1 pinch baking powder
125 g/4½ oz (⅝ cup) sugar
3 drops vanilla essence
in 1 tablespoon sugar
3 yolks of medium eggs
200 g/7 oz cold butter
or margarine
125 g/5 oz blanched ground almonds

For dusting:
about 50 g/2 oz (scant ½ cup) icing (confectioner's) sugar
3 drops vanilla essence
in 1 tablespoon sugar

Per piece:
P: 1 g, F: 3 g, C: 4 g,
kJ: 186, kcal: 44

Tips: If the dough becomes too soft during the preparation, put it in the refrigerator for a little while.
Instead of sprinkling the crescents with icing sugar they can be rolled in caster sugar.

Coconut macaroons

Preparation time:
about 25 minutes

Baking time:
about 25 minutes
per baking sheet;

about 80 pieces/about
2 baking sheets

For the baking sheet:
baking parchment

For the egg white mixture:
200 g/7 oz desiccated coconut
whites of 4 medium eggs
200 g/7 oz (1 cup) caster sugar
1 pinch ground cinnamon
1 drop almond essence

Per piece:
P: 1 g, F: 2 g, C: 3 g,
kJ: 110, kcal: 26

1 Preheat the oven. Line the baking sheet with baking parchment.

2 Roast the desiccated coconut on the baking sheet until light brown and slide onto a large plate to cool down.

3 Whisk the egg whites with a hand mixer with whisk at the highest setting until they form stiff peaks. Quickly whisk in the sugar, cinnamon and flavouring little by little at the highest setting and carefully fold in the roasted desiccated coconut. Using 2 teaspoons, spoon small blobs of stiffened egg white onto the baking sheet and put the baking sheet in the oven **for about 25 minutes**.

Top/bottom heat: about 140 °C/275 °F (preheated), Fan oven: about 120 °C/250 °F (preheated), Gas mark 1 (preheated).

4 Slide the macaroons, still on the baking parchment, off the baking sheet onto a rack to cool down.

Christmas almond splinters

Preparation time:
about 30 minutes,
excluding cooling time;

about 50 pieces

For the baking sheet:
baking parchment

For the almond mixture:
200 g/7 oz blanched flaked
almonds
50 g/2 oz candied orange peel
300 g/10 oz plain chocolate
or full milk chocolate
2 tablespoons zest of untreated
orange
½ teaspoon ground ginger,
or 1 pinch each cinnamon,
cloves, coriander (all ground)

Per piece:
P: 1 g, F: 4 g, C: 4 g,
kJ: 235, kcal: 56

1 Roast the flaked almonds in a pan without fat until golden yellow (photograph 1) and leave on a plate to cool down. Meanwhile, finely chop the candied orange peel. Line the baking sheet with baking parchment.

2 Coarsely chop the chocolate and melt in a bain-marie over low heat, stirring continuously. Stir in the candied orange peel and ginger. Incorporate the almonds and candied orange peel (photograph 2) and, using 2 teaspoons, make small heaps of this chocolate-almond mixture on the prepared baking sheet (photograph 3).

3 Put the almond splinters on the baking sheet and refrigerate until the chocolate has set.

Christstollen (Christmas stollen)

Preparation time:
about 35 minutes, excluding
soaking and rising time

Baking time:
about 50 minutes;

about 16 pieces

For the baking sheet:
baking parchment

For the yeast dough:
200 g/7 oz raisins
100 g/3½ oz currants
100 ml/3½ fl oz (½ cup) rum
375 g/13½ oz (3¾ cups) plain
(all-purpose) flour
1 packet (42 g) fresh yeast
50 g/1¾ oz (4 table-spoons)
sugar
100 ml/3½ fl oz (½ cup) warm
milk
3 drops vanilla essence
in 1 tablespoon sugar
1 pinch salt
1 pinch each cinnamon,
cardamom, ginger, coriander,
cloves, mace (all ground)
2 medium eggs
175 g/6 oz (⅞ cup) soft butter
or margarine
100 g/3½ oz candied orange
peel
100 g/3½ oz candied lemon
peel
100 g/3½ oz blanched ground
almonds

For coating and dusting:
75 g/2½ oz (⅜ cup) butter
some icing (confectioner's) sugar

Per piece:
P: 5 g, F: 18 g, C: 42 g,
kJ: 1532, kcal: 366

1 Put the raisins and currants in the rum and leave to soak overnight.

2 The following day, sift the flour in a mixing bowl and make a well in the middle. Crumble the yeast into it, add 1 teaspoon of the sugar and pour the warm milk on top. Carefully stir in a little of the flour from the edge, using a fork, and let stand for about 15 minutes at room temperature.

3 Add the rest of the sugar, vanilla sugar, salt, spices, eggs and butter or margarine and stir together with a hand mixer with kneading hook, first briefly at the lowest setting, then at the highest setting for about 5 minutes until the dough is smooth.

4 Briefly knead the candied orange and lemon peel, almonds and soaked raisins and currants into the dough on a lightly floured work surface. Cover the dough and leave to rise in a warm place until it has visibly increased in volume. Line the baking sheet with a triple layer of baking parchment.

5 Preheat the oven. Shape the dough into a stollen. To do this, roll out the dough to make a rectangle (about 30 x 25 cm / 12 x 10 in). Roll up the dough starting with the long side and make a depression lengthways using the rolling pin. Fold the left side onto the right side to create a staggered effect. Using your hands, mould the centre of the stollen lengthways into a "bulge". Put the stollen onto the prepared baking sheet and put in a warm place to rise again until it has visibly increased in volume. Put the baking sheet in the oven **for about 50 minutes** and alter the temperature as indicated below.

Top/bottom heat: preheat to about 250 °C/500 °F, bake at about 160 °C/325 °F, Fan oven: preheat to about 220 °C/425 °F, bake at about 140 °C/275 °F, Gas: preheat to mark 9, bake at Gas mark 2–3.

6 Melt the butter and coat the warm stollen with it. Put the stollen on a rack to cool down and dust with icing (confectioner's) sugar.

White bread

Preparation time:
about 20 minutes,
excluding rising time

Baking time:
about 45 minutes

For a rectangular tin or bread
tin (30 x 11 cm / 12 x 4½ in):
some fat
breadcrumbs

For the yeast dough:
100 ml / 3½ fl oz (½ cup) milk
500 g / 18 oz plain (all-purpose)
flour
1 packet fast action dried yeast
1 level teaspoon sugar
1 slightly heaped teaspoon salt
2 medium eggs
yolk of 1 medium egg
150 g / 5 oz crème fraîche

In all:
P: 79 g, F: 74 g, C: 373 g,
kJ: 10404, kcal: 2493

1 Warm the milk for the dough. Sift the flour into a mixing bowl, add the dried yeast and mix carefully. Now add the other ingredients for the dough including the warm milk (photograph 1) and stir quickly into the mixture with a hand mixer with kneading hook, first at the lowest setting, then at the highest setting for about 5 minutes to make a smooth dough (photograph 2). Cover the dough and put in a warm place to rise until it has visibly increased in volume. Grease the bread tin and sprinkle with breadcrumbs.

2 Preheat the oven top and bottom. Knead the dough again briefly, put in the prepared tin and return to a warm place to rise again until it has visibly increased in volume.

3 Make an incision lengthways 1 cm / ⅜ in deep along the top of the bread, using a sharp knife and without pressing down (photograph 3). Brush some water over it and put the tin on a shelf in the oven **for about 45 minutes**.

Top/bottom heat: about 180 °C / 350 °F (preheated), Fan oven: about 160 °C / 325 °F (preheated), Gas mark 4 (preheated).

4 Take the bread out of the tin and put on a rack to cool down.

Variation: You can make white bread with raisins by kneading 150 g / 5 oz raisins into the dough.

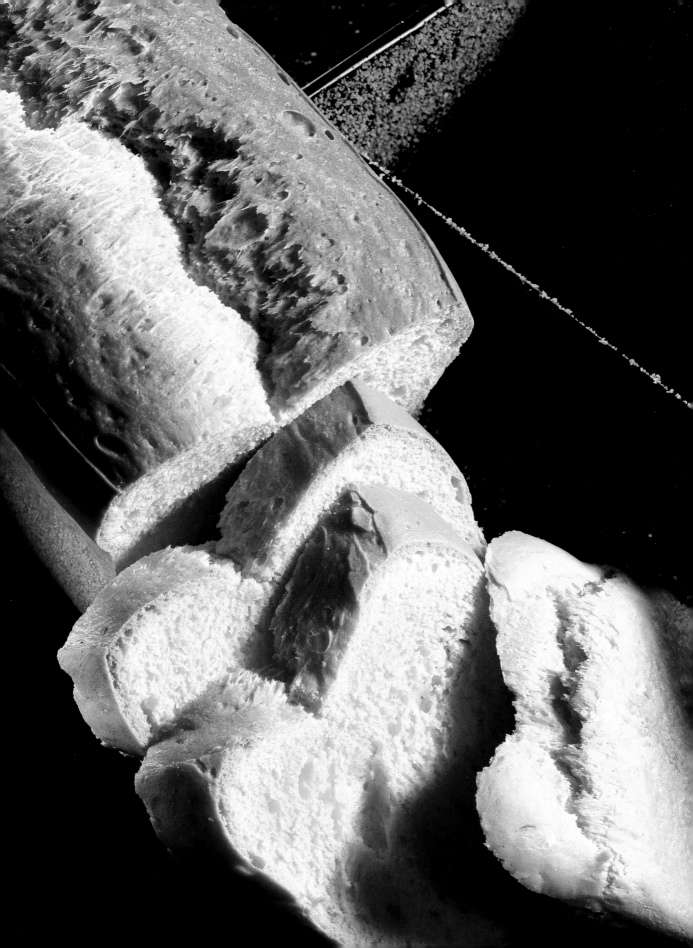

Rye bread
with pumpkin seeds

Preparation time:
about 30 minutes,
excluding rising time

Baking time:
about 40 minutes

For the baking sheet:
baking parchment

For the yeast dough:
250 g/9 oz coarsely ground
wholemeal rye flour
250 g/9 oz (2½ cups) plain (all-
purpose) white flour
1 packet fast action dried yeast
1 level teaspoon sugar
1 level teaspoon salt
375 ml/12 fl oz (1½ cups) warm
water
150 g/5 oz pumpkin seed

In all:
P: 90 g, F: 75 g, C: 352 g,
kJ: 10300, kcal: 2459

1 To make the dough, put the wholemeal rye flour and wheat flour in a mixing bowl, add the dried yeast and mix carefully. Add the other ingredients for the dough (except for the pumpkin seeds) and stir with a hand mixer with kneading hook, first briefly at the lowest setting, then at the highest setting for 5 minutes to make a smooth dough. Incorporate the pumpkin seeds right at the end. Cover the dough and put in a warm place until it has visibly increased in volume. Line the baking sheet with baking parchment.

2 Preheat the oven at the top and bottom. Dust the dough lightly with flour, remove from the bowl and knead briefly on the work surface. Shape the dough into 1 or 2 oval loaves, place on the baking sheet and again leave in a warm place until it has visibly increased in volume. Brush the dough with water and dust with flour. Put the baking sheet in the oven **for about 30 minutes**.

Top/bottom heat: about 200 °C/400 °F (preheated), Fan oven: about 180 °C/350 °F (not preheated), Gas mark 6 (not preheated)

3 Put the bread on a rack to cool down.

Tip: Instead of pumpkin seeds you can also use sunflower seeds.

COOKING – BEST RECIPES

SOUPS

Chicken stock 16
Goulash soup 18
Pea soup with little sausages 20
Cream of trout soup 20
Cream of asparagus soup 22
Thuringian vegetable soup 24
Cheese and leek soup 26
Vegetable noodle soup 28
Cream of vegetable soup (basic recipe) 30
Cream of broccoli soup 30
Cream of carrot soup 30
Cream of pumpkin soup 30
Cream of pea soup. 30
Cream of potato soup 32
Unripe spelt grain soup 32

THICK SOUPS

Old German potato soup 34
Pichelsteiner (meat and vegetable soup) 36
Soup with green beans 38

MEAT

Boiled beef (Tafelspitz) 40
Beef olives (Rouladen) 42
Sauerbraten (braised beef marinated in
    vinegar and herbs) 44
Saxony onion stew 46
Züricher Geschnetzeltes (thin strips of meat
    cooked in sauce) 48
Pork escalopes (Schnitzel) 50
Cured rib of pork, Kassel style 52
Knuckle of pork 54

POULTRY

Chicken fricassée 56
Stuffed goose 58
Chicken legs 60

GAME

Saddle of venison, Baden style 62
Haunch of venison 64
Venison ragout 66
Pheasant with sauerkraut and wine 68

FISH & SEAFOOD

Truite à la meunière 70
Salmon trout with leaf spinach 70
Plaice with bacon 72
Herring fillets, home-made style 74
Smoked fish mousse 74
Marinated salmon 76
Mussels cooked in wine 78

SAUCES

Frankfurt green sauce 80
Cheese sauce 80
Mushroom sauce 82
Mayonnaise 84

VEGETABLES

Parsnip and carrot medley 86
Kohlrabi 86
Green beans 88
Petit pois (peas) 88
Stuffed peppers 90
Celeriac escalopes 92
Shallots in red wine 92

Hunter's cabbage 94

Sauerkraut 94

Cabbage beef olives 96

Brussels sprouts 98

Red cabbage 98

Ceps 100

Mushroom in cream sauce 100

SALADS

Rocket with Parmesan 102

Chinese cabbage with fromage frais 102

Mixed green salad 104

Carrot and apple salad 106

Green bean salad 106

Tomato and onion salad 108

Pork sausage and cheese salad 110

Egg salad with leeks 110

Potato salad with mayonnaise 112

Warm potato salad 112

POTATOES, RICE & PASTA

Potatoes boiled in their skins 114

Boiled potatoes 114

Potato pancakes 116

Potato purée 118

Half-and-half potato dumplings 120

Raw potato dumplings 120

Schupfnudeln (potato noodles) 122

Kastenpickert (yeast potato bread) 124

Spätzle 126

Maultaschen (stuffed Swabian pockets) . . . 128

Breadcrumb dumplings 130

BAKED DISHES

Potato bake 132

Pancake gratin 134

Rice and vegetable gratin 136

EGG & CURD CHEESE DISHES

Stuffed eggs 138

Boiled eggs 140

Eggs with mustard sauce 140

Pancakes 142

SNACKS

Pork fillet toast with cheese 144

DESSERTS

Bavarian pudding 146

Semolina pudding 148

Swiss rice 150

Frothy wine sauce 150

Curd cheese with fruit 152

Baked apples 152

Red fruit pudding 154

Fruit salad 156

Raspberry sorbet 158

Lemon pudding 160

Vanilla sauce 160

BAKING – BEST RECIPES

CAKE MIXTURE

Bergische Waffeln (Bergisch waffles) 164

Crème fraîche waffles 164

Baumkuchen (Layered cake) 166

Nut cake 168

Frankfurter Kranz 170

Marble cake 172

Lemon, cheese and cream torte 174

Maulwurftorte ("Mole cake") 176

Lemon cake 178

ALL-IN-ONE CAKE MIXTURE

Fruit tart 180

Quick plum cake 182

Raspberry and yogurt cake 184

SHORTCRUST PASTRY

Nut triangles 186

Leipziger Lerchen (typical Saxon speciality) . . 188

Berliner Bobbes (typical Berlin speciality) . . . 190

Cheesecake with crumble 192

Friesische Streuseltorte (Friesian crumble torte) 194

Cherry crumble cake 196

Angels' eyes 198

Covered apple pie 200

YEAST DOUGH

Custard snails 202

Mohnstriezel 204

Feiner Gugelhupf 206

Streuselkuchen aus Thüringen
   (Thuringian crumb cake) 208

Butter cake 210

Bienenstich 212

SPONGE MIXTURE

Lüneburger Buchweizentorte
   (Lüneburger buckwheat fancy cake) 214

Schwarzwälder Kirschtorte
   (Black Forest cherry gâteau) 216

Almond and cherry cake 218

Mandarin orange and cheese slices 220

CHEESE AND OIL CAKE MIXTURE

Rolled slices (Coffee slices) 222

Cheese and apple with crumble 224

STRUDEL

Cheese strudel 226

Apfelstrudel (Apple strudel) 228

PUFF PASTRY

Schillerlocken (Cream horns) 230

Crispy cushion pastries 232

PASTRIES FRIED IN FAT

Doughnuts (Berliner) 234

Eberswald fritters (Spritzkuchen) 236

CHRISTMAS PASTRY

Cinnamon stars 238

Vanilla crescents 240

Coconut macaroons 242

Christmas almond splinters 242

Christstollen (Christmas stollen) 244

BREAD

White bread 246

Rye bread with pumpkin seeds 248

A

Almond and cherry cake 218
Angels' eyes 198
Apfelstrudel (Apple strudel) 228
Apples, baked 152
Apple pie, covered 200

B

Baked apples 152
Baumkuchen (Layered cake) 166
Bavarian pudding 146
Beef, boiled (Tafelspitz). 40
Beef olives (Rouladen) 42
Bergische Waffeln (Bergisch waffles) 164
Berliner Bobbes (typical Berlin speciality) . . . 190
Bienenstich 212
Black Forest cherry gâteau
    (Schwarzwälder Kirschtorte) 216
Boiled beef (Tafelspitz). 40
Boiled eggs 140
Boiled potatoes 114
Breadcrumb dumplings 130
Brussels sprouts 98
Butter cake 210

C

Cabbage beef olives 96
Carrot and apple salad 106
Celeriac escalopes 92
Ceps 100
Cheese and apple with crumble 224
Cheese and leek soup 26
Cheesecake with crumble 192

Cheese sauce 80
Cheese strudel 226
Cherry crumble cake 196
Chicken fricassée 56
Chicken legs 60
Chicken stock 16
Chinese cabbage with fromage frais 102
Christmas alomond splinters 242
Christstollen (Christmas stollen) 244
Cinnamon stars 238
Coconut macaroons 242
Coffee slices (Rolled slices) 222
Covered apple pie 200
Cream of asparagus soup 22
Cream of broccoli soup 30
Cream of carrot soup 30
Cream of pea soup. 30
Cream of potato soup 32
Cream of pumpkin soup 30
Cream of trout soup 20
Cream of vegetable soup (basic recipe) 30
Crème fraîche waffles 164
Crispy cushion pastries 232
Curd cheese with fruit 152
Cured rib of pork, Kassel style 52
Cushion pastries, crispy. 232
Custard snails 202

D

Doughnuts (Berliner) 234

E

Eberswald fritters (Spritzkuchen) 236
Egg salad with leeks 110

Eggs, boiled 140

Eggs, stuffed 138

Eggs with mustard sauce 140

F

Feiner Gugelhupf 206

Fish mousse, smoked 74

Frankfurt green sauce 80

Frankfurter Kranz 170

Friesische Streuseltorte

   (Friesian crumble torte) 194

Frothy wine sauce 150

Fruit salad 156

Fruit tart 180

G

Goose, stuffed 58

Goulash soup 18

Green bean salad 106

Green beans 88

Green salad, mixed 104

H

Half-and-half potato dumplings 120

Haunch of venison 64

Herring fillets, home-made style 74

Hunter's cabbage 94

K

Kastenpickert (yeast potato bread) 124

Knuckle of pork 54

Kohlrabi 86

L

Leipziger Lerchen

   (typical Saxon speciality) 188

Lemon cake 178

Lemon pudding 160

Lemon, cheese and cream torte 174

Lüneburger Buchweizentorte

   (Lüneburger buckwheat fancy cake) 214

M

Mandarin orange and cheese slices 220

Marble cake 172

Marinated salmon 76

Maultaschen (stuffed Swabian pockets) . . . 128

Maulwurftorte ("Mole cake") 176

Mayonnaise 84

Mixed green salad 104

Mohnstriezel 204

Mushroom in cream sauce 100

Mushroom sauce 82

Mussels cooked in wine 78

N

Nut cake 168

Nut triangles 186

O

Old German potato soup 34

P

Pancake gratin 134

Pancakes 142

Parsnip and carrot medley 86

Pea soup with little sausages 20

Peppers, stuffed 90

Petit pois 88

Pheasant with sauerkraut and wine 68

Pichelsteiner (meat and vegetable soup) . . . 36

Plaice with bacon 72

Plum cake, quick 182

Pork escalopes (Schnitzel) 50

Pork fillet toast with cheese 144

Pork sausage and cheese salad 110

Potato bake 132

Potato pancakes 116

Potato purée 118

Potato salad, warm 112

Potato salad with mayonnaise 112

Potatoes, boiled 114

Potatoes boiled in their skins 114

Q

Quick plum cake 182

R

Raspberry and yogurt cake 184

Raspberry sorbet 158

Raw potato dumplings 120

Red cabbage 98

Red fruit pudding 154

Rice and vegetable gratin 136

Rocket with Parmesan 102

Rolled slices (Coffee slices) 222

Rye bread with pumpkin seeds 248

S

Saddle of venison, Baden style 62

Salmon, marinated 76

Salmon trout with leaf spinach 70

Sauerbraten (braised beef marinated
   in vinegar and herbs) 44

Sauerkraut 94

Saxony onion stew 46

Schillerlocken (Cream horns) 230

Schnitzel (pork escalopes) 50

Schupfnudeln (potato noodles) 122

Schwarzwälder Kirschtorte
   (Black Forest cherry gâteau) 216

Semolina pudding 148

Shallots in red wine 92

Smoked fish mousse 74

Soup with green beans 38

Spätzle 126

Streuselkuchen aus Thüringen
   (Thuringian crumb cake) 208

Stuffed eggs 138

Stuffed goose 58

Stuffed peppers 90

Swiss rice 150

T

Thuringian vegetable soup 24

Tomato and onion salad 108

Truite à la meunière 70

U

Unripe spelt grain soup 32

V

Vanilla crescents 240

Vanilla sauce 160

Vegetable noodle soup 28

Venison ragout 66

W

Warm potato salad 112

White bread 246

Wine sauce, frothy 150

Z

Züricher Geschnetzeltes (thin strips of meat
   cooked in sauce) 48

Environmental information:	This book and its cover were printed on chlorine-free bleached paper. The shrinkwrapping to protect it from getting dirty is made from environmentally-friendly, recyclable polyethylene material.
Note:	If you have any suggestions, proposals or questions concerning our books, please call us on the following number: +49 521 520651 or write to us: Dr. Oetker Verlag KG, Am Bach 11, 33602 Bielefeld, Germany.
Copyright:	© 2006 by Dr. Oetker Verlag KG, Bielefeld
Editing:	Sabine Puppe, Carola Reich
Translation:	Rosetta Translations, London
Recipe development and consultancy:	Dr. Oetker Versuchsküche, Bielefeld Annette Elges, Bielefeld Anke Rabeler, Berlin
Nutritional calculator:	NutriService GbR, Hennef
Cover photograph:	Thomas Diercks, Hamburg
Photographs in the book:	Thomas Diercks, Hamburg (pp. 19, 21, 23, 27, 29, 39, 41, 51, 55, 59, 62, 67, 69, 77, 89, 93, 97, 101, 107, 109, 113, 115, 117, 119, 123, 131, 135, 137, 141, 143, 149, 155, 161, 168, 169, 171, 185, 201, 205, 233) Ulli Hartmann, Bielefeld (pp. 17, 26, 31, 57, 61, 78, 79, 81, 85, 95, 103, 105, 111, 122, 130, 145, 147, 148, 153, 159) Ulrich Kopp, Sindelfingen (pp. 35, 183, 227) Kramp & Gölling, Hamburg (pp. 219, 229) Bernd Lippert, Bielefeld (pp. 49, 63, 245) Christiane Pries, Borgholzhausen (pp. 71, 116, 133) Norbert Toelle, Bielefeld (pp. 26, 36, 37, 43, 52, 65, 66, 75, 91, 173, 181, 188, 195, 211, 222, 223, 235, 246) Brigitte Wegner, Bielefeld (pp. 14/15, 24, 25, 33, 36, 45, 46, 47, 62, 72, 73, 83, 87, 99, 104, 121, 124, 125, 126, 127, 129, 138, 139, 151, 162/163, 165, 167, 175, 176, 177, 179, 187, 189, 191, 192, 193, 197, 198, 199, 200, 203, 204, 207, 208, 209, 210, 213, 215, 216, 221, 225, 230, 231, 236, 237, 239, 240, 241, 243, 247)
Graphic concept and design: Cover design:	Gaby Herbrecht, Mindelheim kontur:design, Bielefeld
Reproduction: Printing and binding:	Repro Schmidt, Dornbirn, Austria; MOHN Media, Gütersloh Appl, Wemding

The authors have produced this book to the best of their knowledge and belief. All the recipes, tips and advice have been carefully selected and tested. The publishers, employees and author's accept no liability for any loss, damage or injury to people, objects or property that may occur.

ISBN 3–7670–0598–1